IT'S A BRAVE YOUNG WORLD

by **Anu Adebogun**

Illustrated by
Soofiya
& Lila Cruz

Compiled with the help and advice of Dr Roisin Ryan (GP), Beth Cox (Beth Cox Inclusion Consultancy Ltd) and Mary Butler (youth worker).

The world is an ever-changing place and the people within it are capable of incredible things; discoveries are made, records are broken, new facts are found and history recovered. We will be happy to revise and update information in future editions.

LITTLE TIGER
LONDON

LITTLE TIGER
An imprint of Little Tiger Press Limited
www.littletiger.co.uk
1 Coda Studios, 189 Munster Road, London SW6 6AW
Imported into the EEA by Penguin Random House Ireland,
Morrison Chambers, 32 Nassau Street, Dublin D02 YH68
First published in Great Britain 2025
Text copyright © Anu Adebogun 2025
Illustrations copyright © Soofiya and Lila Cruz 2025
Illustrations on pp. 4, 5, 8, 32, 40, 41, 43,
46, 52, 53, 54, 55, 58, 59, 60, 78, 84, 116, 136, 161,
170, 186, 204, 211 copyright © Shutterstock.com 2025
A CIP catalogue record for this book
is available from the British Library
All rights reserved • Printed in China
ISBN: 978-1-83891-640-4
CPB/1800/2768/0824
2 4 6 8 10 9 7 5 3 1

The Forest Stewardship Council® (FSC®)
is a global, not-for-profit organisation dedicated
to the promotion of responsible forest management
worldwide. FSC® defines standards based on agreed
principles for responsible forest stewardship
that are supported by environmental,
social and economic stakeholders.
To learn more, visit www.fsc.org

IT'S A BRAVE YOUNG WORLD

To the person reading this right now,
this book is dedicated to you.
The world that demands so much
of you must do better by you.

You are WORTHY.

Contents

My Story 6

Chapter 1 – Identity — 8

Chapter 2 – Family — 32

Chapter 3 – Friendships — 46

Chapter 4 – Relationships and Self-love — 60

Chapter 5 – Mind, Mood and Feelings — 84

Chapter 6 – School — 116

Chapter 7 – Beliefs — 136

Chapter 8 – The Internet — 170

Chapter 9 – Your Safety — 186

Chapter 10 – Future You — 204

Useful Resources 214

Acknowledgements 216

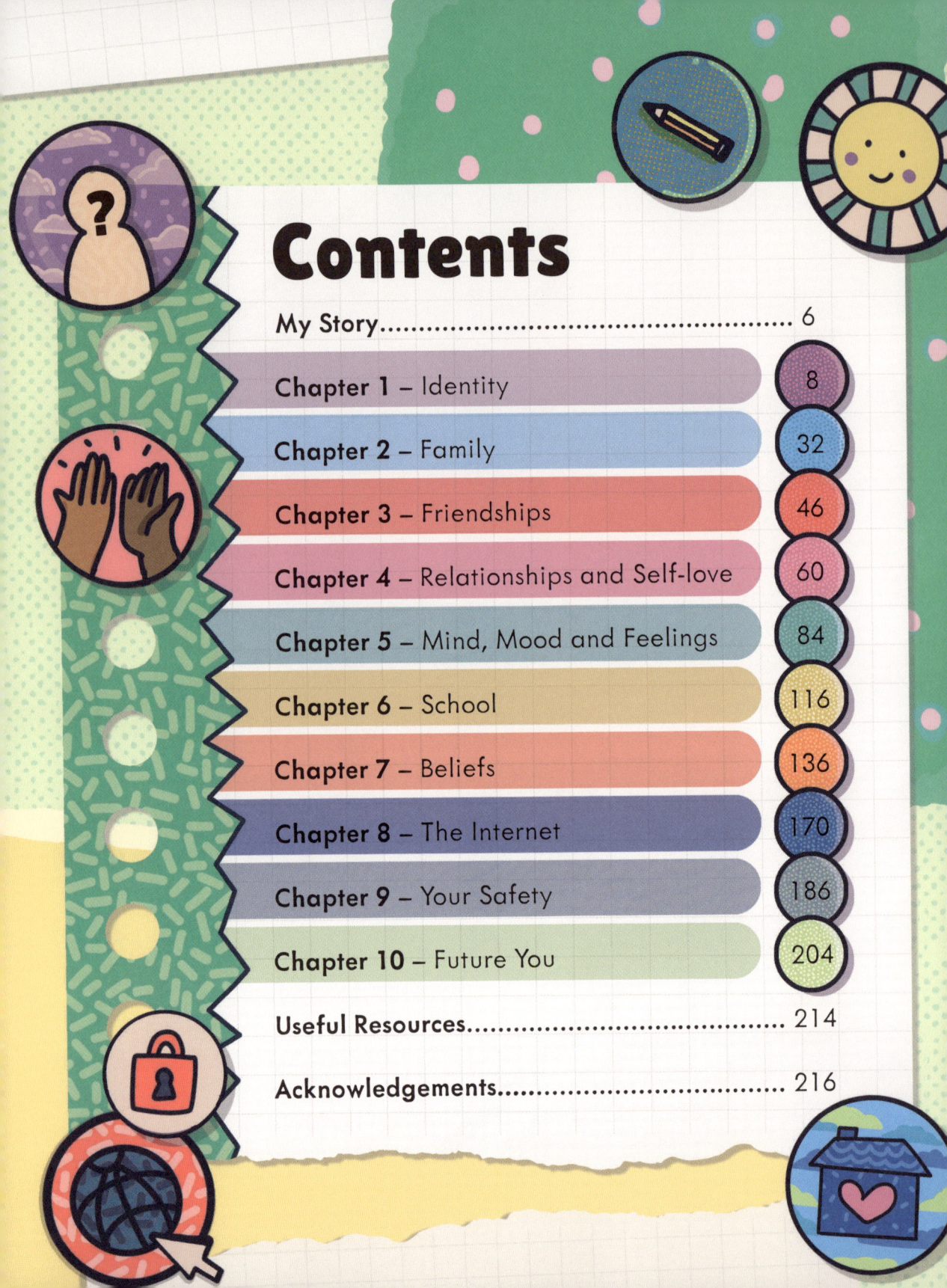

Welcome

Hello! I am so glad you decided to pick up this book. It was written for you, to be an honest companion as you work through the complexities of finding yourself and growing up in today's world. You might be wondering a bit about who I am and why I decided to write this book . . .

My name is Anu Adebogun, and I am an author, youth practitioner and PhD researcher at the University of Oxford looking at issues of gender, justice and crime. Over the years, I have had the immense privilege of delivering sessions to thousands of young people to promote safety, wellbeing and access to education. I also work with several charities and community projects that empower young people.

To say that I am committed to youth development is putting it lightly. I want to see you thrive, step into your power and light up our world. Through my work, I have listened to young people share their struggles with social media, families, friends, school, relationships and so much more. I believe YOU are the future and that is why I wrote this book.

Think of these pages as a journey to get to know yourself better and uncover the power of being brave. Each section covers a different topic, from values and beliefs to healthy boundaries and coping with challenging feelings. You'll find tips on relationships and consent, talking about cancel culture, navigating school and staying safe online – no conversation is off the table.

This book is for you if anything we cover feels relevant, regardless of your gender, age or race. We address some difficult topics but aim to equip you with the information and language to call out unsafe situations. This book will help you stand up for yourself and for others. Use it to become a global citizen and the best version of yourself. I am rooting for you!

ANU x

My Story

I was certainly one of the 'early bloomers', and by early I mean really early (I started my period at nine years old). So while my friends were still playing 'it' in the playground, I had more pressing issues on my mind, like trying not to leak out of my school skirt . . . It felt like I went from Reception to training bra without much space just to be a child.

I still remember my first 'talk' with my Nigerian parents after starting my period. They meant well, but the responsibility was placed on me to 'protect myself' from harm. I was told to avoid boys at all costs because if one of them even mistakenly poked my shoulder, I could fall pregnant (not true of course!). I had to act like nothing different was going on in my body and to keep 'hormonal reactions' at bay. There was a lot of shame attached to how 'grown-up' I was becoming. I am Nigerian, and culturally it is believed that if a girl is 'growing too fast', it is probably because she is 'messing around' – if her breasts are 'too big for her age', it is because she is allowing someone to touch them. I was always confused and hurt by this untrue assumption. It felt like there was no understanding

IT'S A BRAVE YOUNG WORLD

that my body was just on its own unique journey. More importantly, if someone had actually been taking advantage of me as a child, suggesting I was to blame would have caused huge emotional damage. No one should ever be blamed or made to feel ashamed for someone else's inappropriate actions.

From Year Seven onwards, I remember holding my breath as I rushed past the barbershop because the older men inside would almost always make crude remarks. Often, one of the men would come out and follow me down the road, pestering me for my number. When I refused, I would be sworn at for being stuck up.

At this stage, I was none the wiser that this was verbal assault and I could report it. I wish someone had said, "Anu, it's not your responsibility to diminish yourself to stay safe from predators, bullies or abusers." Instead, I was told to hide my growing hips in layers of baggy clothing, to be good enough, quiet enough and to avoid unwanted attention. Rather than being silenced, I wish I had been told about trust and boundaries and taught how to spot the signs of someone violating them.

The responsibility should not be on anyone to make themselves unnoticeable, play it small, avoid the internet or give up the places and activities they enjoy to avoid predators; this only gives more power to abusers. Instead, all of us can be equipped with knowledge and understanding so that we can advocate for ourselves and others. I wish I'd had this guide during my school years and beyond. I hope it is useful to you.

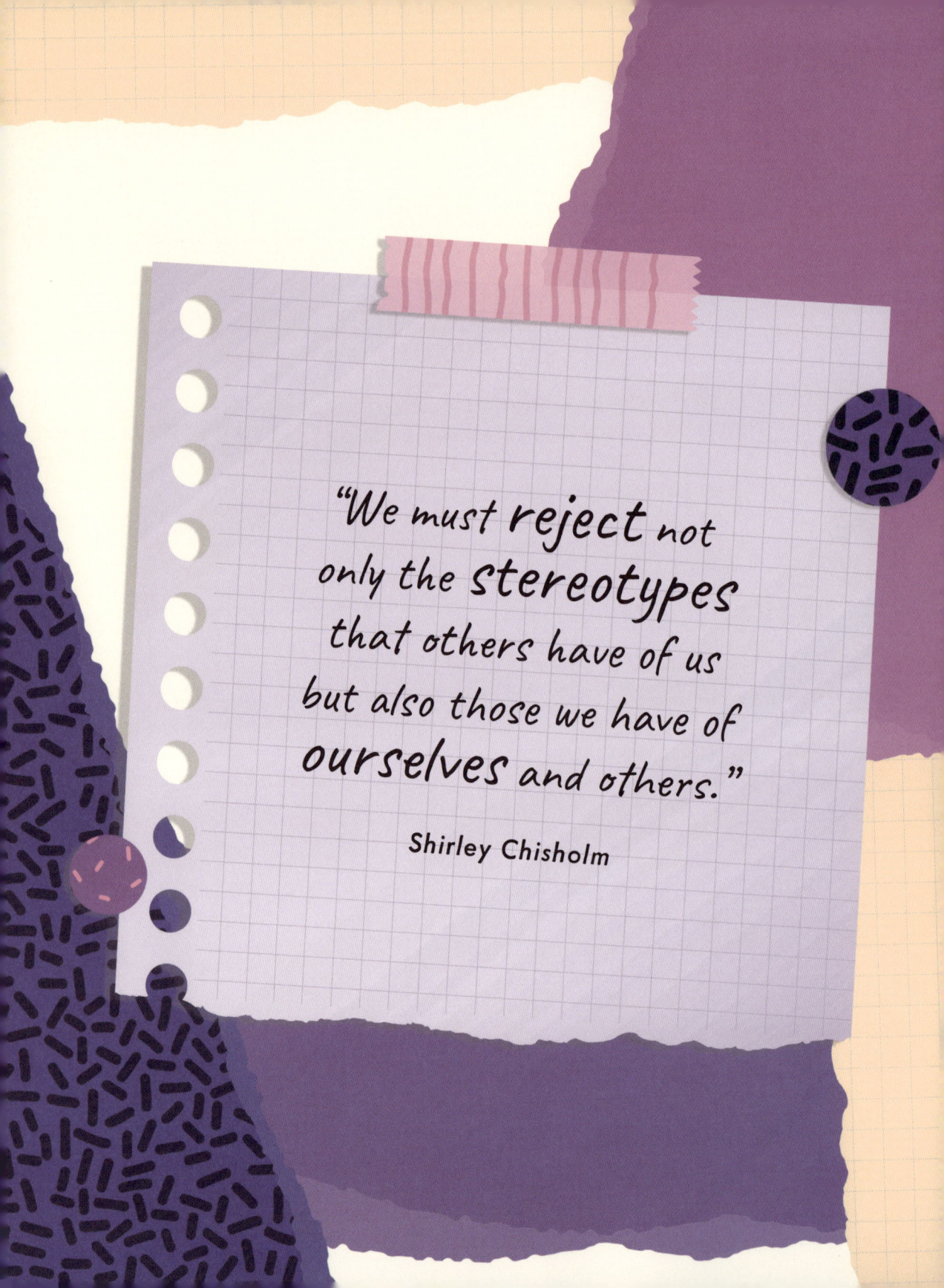

"We must reject not only the stereotypes that others have of us but also those we have of ourselves and others."

Shirley Chisholm

Chapter 1
Identity

Let's explore . . . personal identity, heritage, culture and our strengths and weaknesses.

This book is about YOU – discovering you, honouring you, protecting and celebrating you. Learning who you are sometimes means asking yourself uncomfortable questions and going on a quest to find answers. But we're brave people around here. Being bold and audacious is our way. So let's dive right into the deep work of putting ourselves first and figuring ourselves out.

Who am I? Where do I come from? Am I 'normal'? Why do I do what I do? These are all big questions that EVERYONE will reflect on at some point in their lives and, honestly, will probably have to come back to. That's because your answers will change as you evolve and grow.

When you are born, so many things have already been set for you, such as your family, the country you live in or the colour of your skin. These parts of your identity and background will remain fixed. However, as you grow older you get to know yourself better, and your identity might start to change. Stepping into adolescence means that you can control more of who you are and who you'll become.

This chapter will help you to decide what matters when it comes to defining yourself.

> "If you know me based on who I was a year ago, you don't know me at all. My growth game is strong. Allow me to reintroduce myself."
>
> *Anonymous*

> "When you know
> who you are and what you stand for,
> you stand in WISDOM."
> *Oprah Winfrey*

Making sense of who you are

Identity is such a big part of the human experience, and it can be as complex or simple as you define it to be. Your identity is who you are – all the characteristics, life experiences, opinions and abilities that make you, well, you! Your identity can be shaped by many things, including your gender, race, ethnicity, culture, personality, life experiences and memories.

You might view your bubbly personality as essential to who you are or maybe you're most proud of your creative identity.

Perhaps your cultural identity matters most, and you celebrate it with the way you wear your hair. You may choose to cover your hair because your religious identity takes first place. There are no right or wrong ways to define yourself. This is not a pop quiz **– this is just you getting to know yourself.**

What shapes your identity?

Your identity can be influenced by what's happening on social media or at school or what your family allows (or won't allow). It is not formed in a vacuum but in your community, by doing life with people, by interacting with the world.

> "If I didn't define myself for myself, I would be crunched into other people's fantasies for me and eaten alive."
> *Audre Lorde*

Personal identity refers to the things you choose to define yourself by, like your favourite book, hobby, music or other interests.

Social identity refers to how you define yourself in relation to groups or the traits you share with others. We are often born into these categories; examples include your racial or ethnic background, gender, country of origin, social class or whether you are disabled. Some of these categories can change as you go through life.

Class identity relates to a person's position in society based on their education, wealth or occupation. In the UK, it falls into three basic categories: working class, middle class and upper class. Working-class jobs include retail, office administration, construction or factory work. Middle-class jobs include professions such as law, medicine, banking and politics. Upper-class groups include the royal family and aristocracy (those born with great wealth, status, power or privilege). Social class is an outdated way of creating a hierarchy between individuals and groups. That said, there are many people who take pride in their class identity and the traditions that come with their background.

Disability or neurodiversity

Social identity can also relate to whether someone is disabled or not. Disabilities refer to physical or mental conditions that mean a person faces more barriers in life. Sometimes these barriers are subtle and come from false beliefs that disabled people are not able to do certain things. Other times, the barriers are unmissable, like a building not having wheelchair access or a lack of accessible toilets in public spaces.

Neurodiversity is a concept that recognises that all brains are different and the term 'neurodivergence' is used when a person's cognitive wiring – for example, the way they think, learn, understand, process and remember information – differs from what is considered typical. Some disabled people may not want to view their condition as part of their identity but others may see their condition as a key part of who they are. Claiming it as part of their identity can be a form of empowerment.

Anne Wafula Strike

Anne Wafula Strike had polio as a child and lost all movement in her lower body. Anne was stigmatised and called a snake because initially she had to crawl on the floor to get around. However, in later life she moved to the UK and started wheelchair racing. She began to view her disability as a strength and her wheelchair as an empowering tool in her race for a better life. Anne went on to be a Paralympic wheelchair racer and uses her platform to challenge misconceptions about disability, giving motivational speeches and campaigning for better access for and inclusion of disabled people. She was awarded an MBE in 2014 for services to disability sport and charity.

> "When you have a disability, knowing that YOU ARE NOT defined by it is the sweetest feeling."
>
> Anne Wafula Strike MBE

Gender

Gender refers to the different behaviour and traits that society associates with boys, girls, men and women, while biological sex describes the physical differences between males and females. Gender identity is a term for how people feel about their gender. While it can correspond with the biological sex a person was assigned at birth, others may identify with a gender different to the sex they were registered as. You may feel that your gender is an important part of your identity, or you might feel that there are other more important things that define you. Perhaps you have rejected the idea of gender altogether.

> Understanding or questioning your gender identity can feel isolating and stressful. If you need support and don't feel able to speak to a trusted adult, then check the resources section at the back of the book for help.

Intersectionality

In 1989, a Black scholar named Professor Kimberlé Crenshaw came up with the term 'intersectionality'. Intersectionality describes the way different identities combine within a person, shaping the way they live and experience the world. Professor Crenshaw found that Black women and girls experienced hostility, discrimination and prejudice because of the ways their gender, racial and class identities intersected.

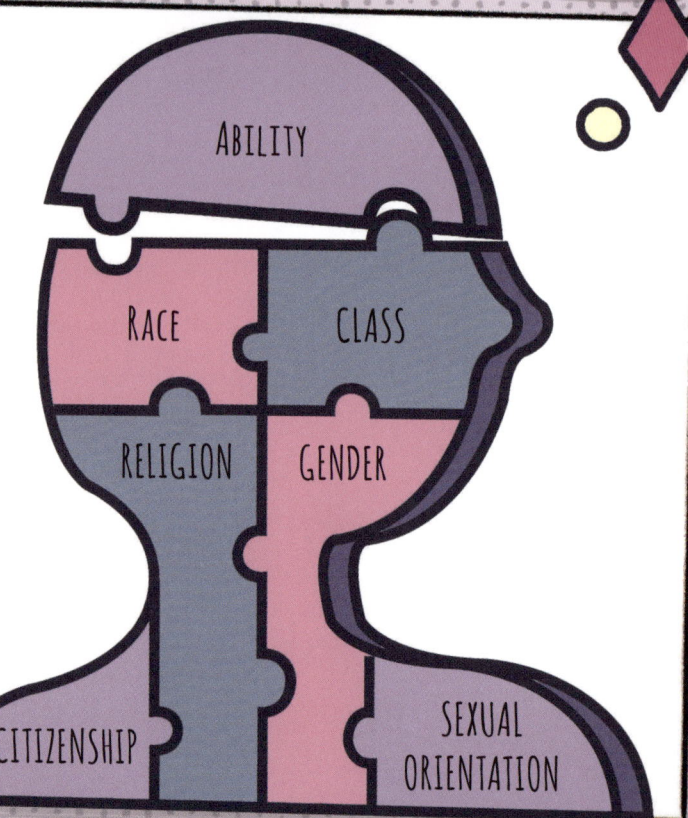

Why the hostility to who I am?

You may find yourself in a society or community that is hostile to intersecting aspects of your personal or social identity. For instance, some Muslim girls who choose to make their religious identity visible by wearing hijabs or burqas suffer Islamophobic abuse (more on this in Chapter 7).

Some people choose to be hostile because of the stereotypes they hold about the identities of others. A stereotype is a simplistic (and sometimes untrue) belief about people or things with a shared characteristic. They can be used to discriminate against individuals or whole communities.

On the flip side, you may also face hostility when it appears that you are showing up in a way that's different to the box you have been put in. Growing up, I remember that Black girls who were into grunge music, wore Dr Marten boots or just had a different vibe from what was expected of them were teased for 'trying to act white'. These girls were punished for presenting themselves in unexpected ways. They were not given the space or respect to explore and embrace their identities.

For example, a gender stereotype could be that boys are assertive and they don't cry, while girls are fragile and obedient.

"No one is born believing in harmful stereotypes. They are learned over time. The good news is they can be unlearned."
Kevin Faulconer

Take a look at these identity wheels.

Use a notebook or journal to create your own identity wheels, then answer the questions.

Do you have **IDENTITIES** that affect how other people see you?

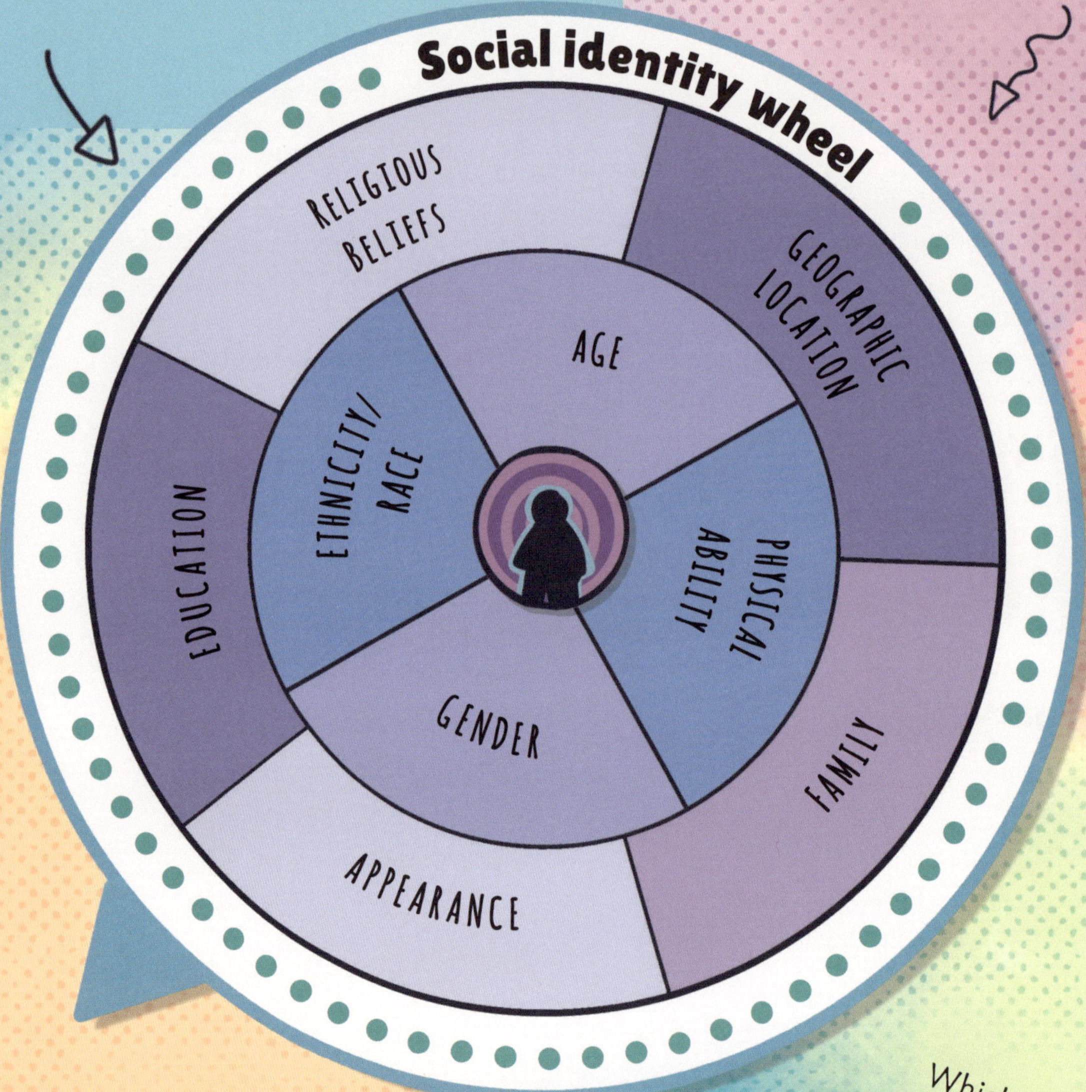

Social identity wheel

- Religious Beliefs
- Geographic Location
- Age
- Physical Ability
- Family
- Appearance
- Gender
- Ethnicity/Race
- Education

Which **IDENTITIES** would you like to know more about?

Which of these **SOCIAL** identities do you think about most?

Which ones don't feel as **RELEVANT** to you?

What part of your personal identity are you most **PROUD** of?

Do you find your **PERSONAL IDENTITY** hard to share with others?

WHY do you think that is?

Are there parts of your identity you want to **KNOW** more about?

Personal identity wheel

- FAVOURITE MUSIC
- BEST SKILL
- FAVOURITE MOVIE
- FAVOURITE BOOK
- FAVOURITE FOOD
- FAVOURITE HOBBY
- FAVOURITE OUTFIT
- PERSONAL MOTTO
- WHO YOU LIVE WITH

In your world, you take centre stage – this is your life and your journey, so you get to be the main character in your narrative. Let's build a main character profile which explores all the aspects of your identity that matter most to YOU. Everyone is different and the emphases we place on our identity will vary; this wheel should be authentic (true to you) and personal.

> "I'm dark-skinned. I'm quirky. I'm shy, I'm strong. I'm guarded. I'm weak at times. I'm sensual. I'm not overtly sexual. I am so many things in so many ways."
>
> Viola Davis

SOMETIMES I FELT 'LESS THAN' FOR DARING TO ASPIRE.

Story time

I know first-hand just how hard it can be to accept and embrace yourself when people choose to be hostile towards your identity. As a Nigerian girl growing up on a council-flat estate in Hackney, London, I was aware of how race, gender and class could shape life experiences and access to opportunities. Even after leaving that environment, when I began studying at a prestigious university, certain aspects of my identity (race and gender) travelled with me. There were times when I felt 'less than' for being in those spaces and daring to aspire.

I remember one experience in particular – I had just finished my law degree and after bagging a first-class honours, I was feeling enthusiastic about my future. I attended a law fair in London and excitedly shared with a top barrister my aspiration to study for a master's in the USA. Now, studying abroad is no light feat and it is really expensive, but there are great scholarships, grants and schemes available. So it was such a big shame (on him) and soul-crushing (for me) to hear him laugh at my goal and tell me that I "must have a very wealthy sugar daddy to dare have such an ambition."

Not only was he ignorant and rude, but by mentioning a 'sugar daddy' he was sexualising me. I remember feeling like his words had slapped me across the face, but I was also painfully aware of the crowded hall and that if I made a scene, I would draw attention to myself as an angry Black girl. I didn't know how to respond, and so I walked away feeling embarrassed and shaken up. It is understandable if you feel unsure or ashamed about aspects of your identity because of other people's hostility. But your identity is sacred, and you have the right to be safe regardless of how society, institutions and other people may feel about you.

REFLECTION

If something like this happens to you, there are ways to take action:

- **Speak directly** to the perpetrator.
- **Share what happened** with a trusted person.
- **Ask an adult** to help you report the incident, or check out the websites on P214–5.
- If you don't feel comfortable speaking up, remember that sometimes bravery is about **being cautious**.

Celebrating your heritage

Where do you come from?

This might sound like a simple question, but if you're like me and have a dual heritage or if you don't know the details of your biological family, it might be harder to respond to. Do you reply based on where your parents are from, where you were born or where you live now? If you live in a country that's different to where your parents were born, it is likely you are 'bi-cultural', meaning you're growing up in a mixed cultural environment. Sociologist Ruth Hill Useem coined the term 'third-culture kid' to describe this experience.

The joys and pains of a dual heritage

Having a dual identity can be enriching – you are likely to be flexible, adaptable and curious about the world. You might speak different languages and feel like a true global citizen. There are benefits to being bi-cultural, but it can sometimes feel like a struggle to fit in – almost like you belong nowhere – and make peace with the different parts of yourself. You may not feel that the culture of those who made or raised you is the same as your own.

> "You don't stumble upon your heritage. It's there, just waiting to be explored and shared."
> Robbie Robertson

Being born in Nigeria and having Nigerian parents means I am very much a girl of the Yoruba tribe. However, moving to the UK aged two and going on to live, study and work there for more than two decades mean that most of my real-world experience has been in the UK rather than Nigeria.

I've only been 'back home' twice, and on a short trip to Nigeria in 2021 my Britishness became an object of scorn. People acted as if they could not understand me, mocked my accent and even said I was faking it. When I got frustrated and tried to speak my mother tongue (Yoruba), I was laughed at for confusing my tenses or saying a phrase that made sense in English but pointed to pure Yoruba illiteracy. On the other hand, growing up in Britain, I got tired of hearing, "No, I mean, where are you really from?" whenever I said I was from east London. Despite living and growing up in Britain, I was made to feel like I had no real claim to this country.

Being Nigerian-British means that my cultural heritage is vast, rich and diverse (if confusing at times). It has shaped who I am today, the decisions I make and the things I enjoy.

Growing up Nigerian meant knowing that my mum's eyes or the pointing of her lips could hold many hidden messages. It meant having to ikunle (kneel or curtsy) to show elders respect, whether at church or the local Primark. It meant preparing the peppers and rodo (scotch bonnet) to make spicy jollof rice and wearing colourful Ankara fabric to attend the large weddings of people I barely knew. Growing up British meant knowing Kickers were the cool school shoes but also knowing my mother wouldn't spend that much on them. It meant watching TV when my dad was at work because he thought some of the shows set a bad example. It meant punctuating every sentence with 'innit' and 'skeen' and wearing neon-coloured shoelaces in my hair.

> The question of where you are from should not be used as proof that you don't belong. It is for you to reflect on and explore, to help you understand and celebrate your culture and heritage.

Culture and heritage

If you and those you live with grew up in the same country, you might feel excluded from this conversation around culture, but you should not. You still have a unique cultural identity shaped by your age, generation and even the city or region you grew up in. This aspect of your identity is worth discovering, owning and celebrating!

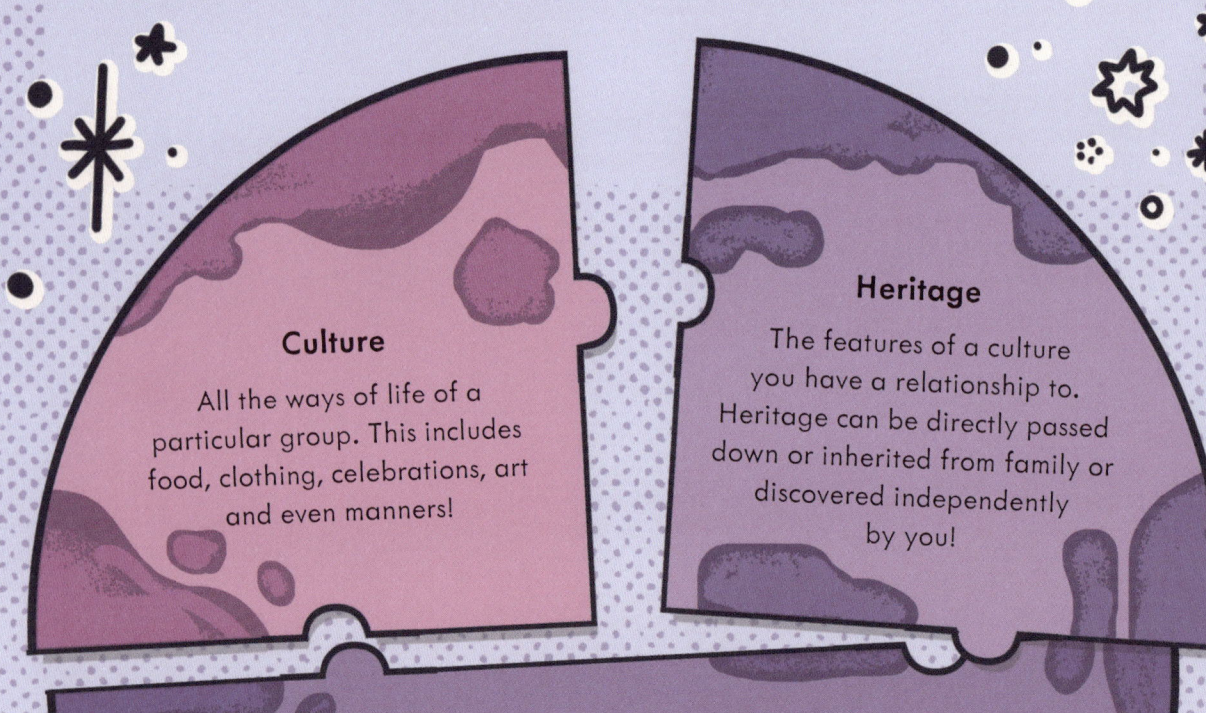

Culture
All the ways of life of a particular group. This includes food, clothing, celebrations, art and even manners!

Heritage
The features of a culture you have a relationship to. Heritage can be directly passed down or inherited from family or discovered independently by you!

Subcultures
You will have your own distinct style of dressing and behaving as well as your own interests and beliefs – this is called a youth subculture. It can help you to explore your identity, express yourself and develop a sense of belonging. For hundreds of years, young people have been defying societal expectations and creating their own subcultures. For example, the 'flappers' were a group of young women in the 1920s who dared to dress and behave in 'shocking' ways – pairing layered pearls with edgy bobs and bold jewellery in revolt against the monochrome style of the time.

Some youth subcultures are shaped by the fashion of previous movements or music genres; examples include hipsters, punks, streetwear gamers, cottagecore or dark academia. If you belong to a youth subculture, think about how this shapes your cultural identity, behaviour and attitude differently to the heritage you share with your family.

JOURNAL TIME
Celebrating your culture

Developing a positive sense of identity means being at peace with your heritage and your culture. It also means being empowered to redefine any negativity; you have that power.

Write down or think about the answers to these questions. If you don't know much about your family, that's okay. You can consider the culture of other people in your life and how that's affected you.

- What does your culture mean to you? Has it changed over time?
- Do any aspects of your culture or heritage make you uncomfortable? If you answered yes, why is that? How could you change this?

The more you learn about your heritage, the more creatively you can celebrate and showcase your cultural pride. Which of these suggestions would help you celebrate your culture?

- Speak your language.
- Explore or wear cultural dress.
- Listen to older people share stories of their childhood.
- Watch films set in your family's culture.
- Watch documentaries that explore your culture.
- Learn to cook food from your culture.
- Attend cultural festivals.
- Visit museums and archives.
- Travel with family.
- Can you think of another suggestion?

Know your strengths!

Growing up is a lot of fun. You may get to define life on your own terms, making decisions about who to hang out with or what clothes to wear. With this growing freedom come worries about fitting in or finding your place in society, but everyone is different and a diversity of personalities and abilities should be celebrated.

> "Courage is the first of human qualities because it is the quality which guarantees the others."
> *Aristotle*

Getting to know yourself is a powerful tool that will help you make better decisions and navigate the independence adolescence brings.

Let's begin with strengths. Do you know yours? Many girls feel like they have to play it small in order to be liked or seen as humble. Which activities are you naturally good at? Sometimes we take for granted how great we are at something because it comes easily. We assume that it must be easy for everyone and therefore not a big deal . . .

. . . BUT IT IS A BIG DEAL. YOU'RE AMAZING!

Involve your community

We can be our own worst critic at times, but when we struggle to see strength in ourselves, our community (those who love and support us) can affirm us. Think of a friend, sibling, mentor, parent or anyone you trust. Ask them to write down three of your strengths and do the same for them, then exchange papers. What did you feel looking at the strengths they identified?

Discover it!

There isn't a single person without any gifts or strengths. But maybe you looked at the box and thought, "Um . . . I'm struggling to see myself as any of these." That's okay; perhaps you know your strengths and just need to give yourself permission to OWN them, or maybe you genuinely struggle to see strength in yourself. Try out some of these exercises to begin the journey of uncovering your self-worth.

It can be eye-opening when we realise that the way other people see us is different to how we see ourselves. Once you've discovered your strengths, own them and get to using them!

Take a strength-finding test

There are loads of online tests you can take to learn more about your personality or to discover your strengths. The VIA character survey is a free, scientific survey of character strengths. Visit **www.viacharacter.org/survey/account/register**

REFLECTION

- What do you enjoy doing?
- What energises you?
- What are you proud of?
- When do you feel most comfortable?

> "If you can dance and be free and not embarrassed, you can rule the world."
> — Amy Poehler

Courage and confidence

Everyone defines strengths differently. In this quote, Amy is referring to the confidence it takes to dance unashamed in front of people. It doesn't matter what those people are thinking. Amy recognises that the courage required to be YOU, no matter the time, place or opinion of others, is a strength that can spur you on to make big moves.

> "The world needs that special gift that only you have."
> — Marie Forleo

Is it really a weakness?

A huge part of self-development and improvement is being able to take feedback and positive criticism. This means we have to open ourselves up to hear hard truths from the people who love us, care about us and want to see us grow – this shows maturity and a growth mindset (meaning you're willing to improve and change). However, don't be too quick to take on the definitions of other people if it seems that they are trying to limit you.

Think about the things you consider to be weaknesses and recognise that they might not be bad in and of themselves. They could be strengths in disguise – maybe you just need to work on applying them differently.

> "My aunties would always say I talked way too much and chide me for asking, 'Why?'"
> Lilian (14)

> "At parents evening, my teachers would say the same thing to my parents: 'She's too bossy and the class always listens to her ideas.'"
> Shola (15)

I remember hearing criticism like this A LOT growing up, and for a long time I felt really bad about myself. I only realised in later life that the weaknesses my teachers saw in me – being 'talkative' or 'bossy' and asking why – were actually great strengths. They showed I could communicate and be inquisitive and confident enough to ask adults questions. Now, I use these strengths in the work I do as a researcher, author and advocate for young people.

We could all use a bit of polishing to shine . . .

A huge part of being brave is the ability to own your strengths but also to recognise when there is room for improvement without feeling ashamed. Some weaknesses really are just that – a weakness or sore point in our personalities. If the weakness hurts you or other people, you can work on it. You aren't fixed in your nature; you can grow and evolve. Give yourself permission to get better.

JOURNAL TIME

1. Weakness or strength?

Here are some examples of perceived weaknesses reframed as strengths.

Weakness . . .
I am bossy.
I am pushy.
I am a chatterbox.

. . . Turned to strength
I am a leader.
I am determined.
I have strong communication skills.

Can you think of some of your own?

2. Embracing weakness

Think of a **particular weakness** that you have.

Do you want to **change** it or **embrace** it?

How could you develop this **weakness** into a **strength**?

BUILD ON YOUR STRENGTHS

If you want to change or challenge this weakness, write down **why**.

It's a journey

It can be hard trying to decide the 'right' things to derive worth, value and a sense of purpose from. While it is important to celebrate your strengths and work on your limitations, this is a balancing act. You are more than the things you do well or the times you've failed. Your value as a human is not tied to your achievements, no matter how impressive they might be.

Hopefully this chapter has got you thinking about your identity, but none of this is written in stone. As you evolve, you might find that what you once considered important for personal and social identity has completely changed. This is a sign that you're growing, and that's something we will always celebrate over here. It is okay to change how you see yourself and how you want the world to see you. One of the exciting and empowering things about being human is the ability to change: your mind, your views, your decisions and your life. To some degree, we will always be on that journey of growth, self-discovery and learning.

The only constant thing is change.

Chapter 2
Family

Let's explore . . . parenting styles, family conflict and sibling relationships.

That said, family can help form who you are and who you go on to be. **So let's get down to business, family business that is.**

Families come in all shapes and sizes. You are born into this weird and wonderful group of people who you did not get to choose. You may share similarities and personal connections, but you are still your own person. Families are never perfect because individual humans aren't perfect. And so when you put a bunch of imperfect people in a house and ask them to 'do life' together, there are bound to be tensions and disagreements!

"Other things may change us, but we **start** and **end** with the **family**."
Anthony Brandt

AU PAIR

FOSTER MUM

UNCLE
(dad's best friend)

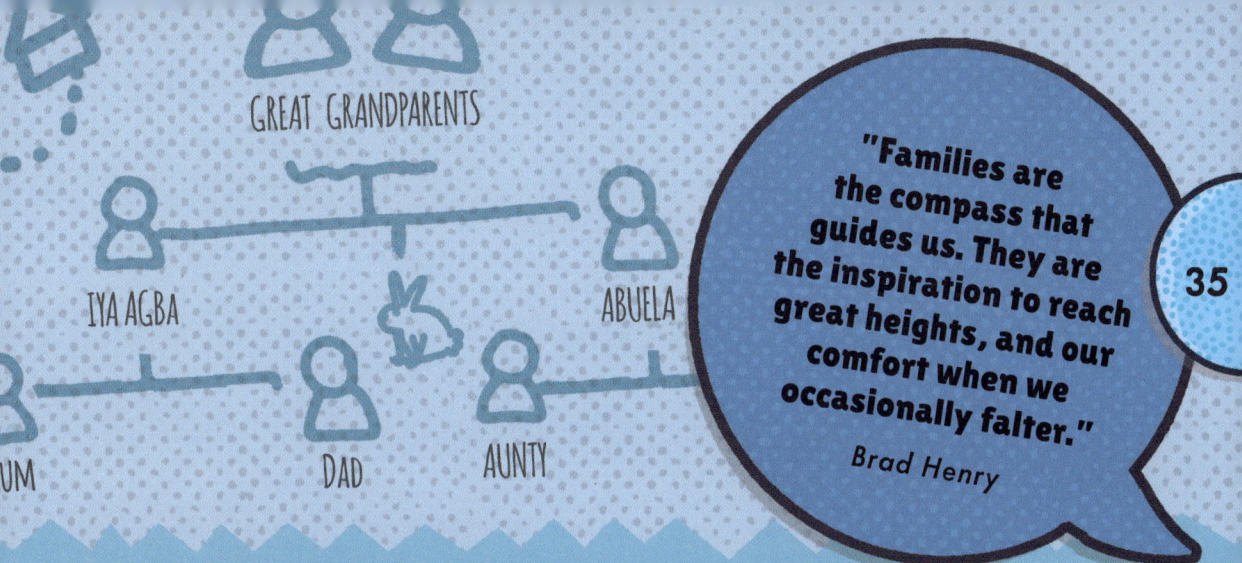

"Families are the compass that guides us. They are the inspiration to reach great heights, and our comfort when we occasionally falter."
Brad Henry

Parents and caregivers

Research has shown that the early relationships and attachments we form (or fail to form) with our caregivers can have a lasting impact on our future relationships. A psychologist called John Bowlby described this as the 'attachment theory'.

Attachments are incredibly important. A child naturally relies on their parent for comfort, food and protection, and many parents will instinctively nurture and provide for their child.

Some parents struggle to provide the love, care and secure attachment a child needs because they did not have these things as a child. However, don't worry if you don't have a strong bond with your parents or if you don't have a consistent caregiver. Studies show that a young person only needs to have a strong attachment to one person who really cares for them to be okay in life. This doesn't need to be a family member; you can create that attachment with mentors or other people you know.

JOURNAL TIME

Welcome to my house

Draw the people and pets that live in your house. Beside each drawing, write one thing you absolutely love about that inhabitant.

What's your parenting story?

No two children are the same. Even biological twins have differences! And so with every new child, parents are having to adjust their parenting styles. Try to show empathy (understanding) towards these adults who are trying their best. They are not perfect but, honestly, neither are we. Most of the time, when a parent says no, they are trying to protect you. Aim to keep this in mind when you next have a disagreement or struggle to understand each other.

Four types of parents

Before you read on, remember that most people do not fit neatly into boxes, but research into psychology, parenting and human behaviour has found that there are four basic types of parents.

1 Permissive

These parents have plenty of time and attention for you. They are easy-going and behave more like friends than parents. They tend not to call you out on your bad behaviour and don't put any expectations on you. As there are no rules, you don't generally feel the need to rebel. But with the lack of expectations and boundaries, it might be hard for you to push yourself or to feel safe, nurtured and cared for.

2 Authoritarian

These parents bring the firm strictness and none of the play. Their focus is making you the most talented pianist, mathematical or literary genius or gold-medal-winning athlete. They are all about rules, boundaries and your exceptional achievement. They love you but they invest a lot in you, and so they are determined to see you succeed.

3 Democratic

These parents have lots of rules but they tell you why the rules exist. They are strict but also give you love, attention and time. Mostly, democratic parents are reasonable, and even you can agree to that!

4 Disengaged

These parents don't seem to care. They may ignore you and can be cold. They don't make rules but when you annoy them they can be harsh with punishments. This type of parenting in particular can become abusive. If this is your parents' attitude, please speak to someone. Turn to p214–5 for a list of organisations you can safely speak to if you find yourself in an unsafe situation at home.

Activity time
Spot your parent type

Have a think about these four parent types. Do you see yours anywhere? If you feel uncomfortable reading this and realise that you are not happy with the way you are being parented, you could try discussing this with them. Maybe you want them to be more affectionate, or maybe you would like the structure of having some more boundaries – let them know how you feel if it's safe to do so.

REFLECTION

Most of us have a story of being parented.
If you do, take a moment to reflect on your experience.
How would you describe it?

Think about how your parents have shaped who you are today.

- Are things great, not so great or somewhere in between?
- Is your privacy respected or are your boundaries tested?
- Are you anxious to please your parents or worried about not meeting their standards?

. . . but pouring from an empty cup does nothing to serve **you**.

REFLECTION

Do you feel that you have to give a lot to those around you?

Are you ever treated differently because of your gender?

Do your answers to the above questions affect how you see yourself?

Remember, **self-love is not selfish** – it's preservation. It's a guide to loving others better and raising the standard of what you expect from them.

Your place in the family

There are quite a few assumptions and stereotypes about the places we occupy within our families, especially around birth order. For example, the **youngest child** is often stereotyped as attention-seeking, **middle children** are thought to be overlooked and rebellious, the **eldest child** is often seen as controlling or as a leader and an **only child** can be labelled as selfish or spoilt. You may have been given a title that put you in a certain box and stopped you from feeling fully 'seen' by your family. Sometimes labels are given fondly or jokingly but they can still be damaging.

Parental pressure

Even if your background is very different to mine, many parents (often with the best intentions) put pressure on their kids to live up to immense expectations, whether that's extra tuition, ballet classes, cello lessons or getting into the best university. This might leave you feeling like a product being shaped to showcase your mum and dad's great parenting. It can be overwhelming and leave you feeling like you could lose your place in the family if you are not 'good enough'.

The quiet one

The smart one

The stubborn one

Were you ever given a title like the above? Did you feel under pressure because of it? Maybe you wanted to try something new or shared an idea only to be told, "We don't do that in this family."

Reflect on the titles you have been given. Have they affected you?

A culture clash

In my work, I have seen that many children grow up with a different sense of identity and values to their parents. This is completely normal – not only are you growing up in a different time and generation, but you were born in the digital age. This book is all about celebrating the fact that you have a voice and equipping you to feel confident using it, whether online or IRL.

Activity time
Spot the culture clash

Here are some examples of cultural clashes between young people and their parents.

What is causing the clashes between the girls and their parents? Do you think their parents are bad people?

Afua is 14 and her twin brothers Kwasi and Kojo are 12. Afua and her mum are constantly arguing about cleaning, cooking and laundry. Afua does not feel comfortable doing the household chores alone and wonders why the boys can't help. Her mum always replies, "You are a girl! I want you to grow up to become a good wife and mother." Afua has tried challenging her mum on this but she does not listen. Afua is beginning to despise her Ghanaian heritage; she thinks it's oppressive towards girls.

As a Muslim, Beren is proud of her religion, but she wants to wait until sixth form to wear the hijab. Her dad is always bringing this up with her and they end up having arguments. He thinks it is shameful that Beren does not wear the hijab and thinks she is 'exposing herself'.

What could Beren do to make her dad **UNDERSTAND** her decision?

How would you **ADVISE** Afua on relating to her mum?

TIPS FOR
resolving conflicts with parents

Pick your battles
Sometimes it can feel easier to let things slide than risk stirring the waters. This approach could be okay for petty issues, but if something is affecting your wellbeing, it is important to talk about it.

Communicate
Giving people the silent treatment might feel good in the moment but it does nothing to resolve the issue. Be willing to have a conversation.

Watch the volume
No one likes being shouted at. Yelling will make an argument worse; your parents will only get defensive.

Timing is everything
It is great that you are open to talking things out with your caregiver but be mindful of when you approach them. If they've come back from work after a long day or just had an argument with someone, that's probably not the best time. Alternatively, you could say, "Something is upsetting me that I'd like to get off my chest. Is now a good time to talk?".

Show empathy
Are your family or caregivers being mean or do they just have a different worldview? Acknowledge their feelings even if you don't agree with them.

Write it out
If you know you'll get flustered in the moment, you could try writing a letter outlining what's bothering you. Putting your thoughts on paper could help you to process things and gives your parent time to reflect before responding.

Siblings

The emotions we feel towards our siblings can be positive or negative – often both! Siblings come with many benefits – studies show that having a brother or sister can make you a healthier, happier person. A loving relationship with your siblings can protect you from feeling lonely or unwanted and can reduce stress, as well as most likely improving your negotiation and communication skills. So siblings can be great but there are bound to be a few rifts!

When we are at home, we typically don't worry as much about being liked or acting polite in the way that we do when we are around friends or strangers. With friends, we care about how we appear and about being accepted. In families, without the social pressure to act nice, we might surprise ourselves with how rude, irritating and unkind we can become.

> "**Siblings** are the people we practise on, the people who **teach** us about fairness and cooperation and kindness and caring – quite often the hard way."
>
> Pamela Dugdale

MY SIBLINGS

big sister (steals my clothes)

little brother (sooooooo annoying)

I ♥ YOU!

The green-eyed monster

Loving your siblings, or at least getting along with them, can be tricky when other people compare you. Remember when I asked if you had ever been given a label like 'the stubborn one' or 'the smart one'? Sometimes these labels and titles come from comparisons between siblings. They can be hurtful and cause siblings to start competing to get in the good graces of their parents, which can lead to jealousy. Your envy might make you want to preserve your sense of self by bossing around your younger siblings so you remain in control. Or you might want to irritate and unnerve the seemingly perfect older sibling so that everyone will see through them. There is no judgement here! While it is a normal part of the human experience, there are ways to tame that green-eyed monster.

JOURNAL TIME
Sibling jealousy

Have you ever felt jealous of your siblings? Are you able to recognise what the triggers were? Was it when your parent got them a gift, praised them for having a talent or took their side in an argument? Note down what the triggers tend to be.

TIPS FOR
managing sibling jealousy

Practise gratitude
Remind yourself of all the things that make you unique and wonderful.

Identify
Find out where the jealousy is coming from.

Voice your concerns
Let your caregivers know if their behaviour is contributing to your jealousy.

Be honest
Recognise that you are feeling jealous but understand that it is a normal feeling you can work on.

Family life

I hope that this chapter has helped you reflect on your home, siblings, place in the family and experiences of being parented. Family life is a messy tangle of different views, personalities and experiences. Your parents are not perfect – neither are your siblings and neither are you. BUT your family must provide a safe space for you to learn, grow, make mistakes and develop your independence.

"Want nothing but the best for your friends, because when your friends are **happy** and **successful**, it's probably going to be easier for you to be happy."

Roxane Gay

Chapter 3
Friendships

Let's explore . . .
friendship labels and values, frenemies, fallouts, peer pressure and breakups.

In ancient times, survival was dependent on fitting in with the rest of the tribe in order to gain food, shelter, protection and companionship. We still have this evolutionary need to find our community and a sense of belonging. This is one of the many reasons that having friends and fitting in can feel like such a big deal at times. Whether you have a massive squad of besties or a small, tight circle, great friendships can make life a little easier.

Friends share our interests and allow us to be ourselves. They make us laugh when we're feeling glum, listen to our worries, think of wild solutions and always remind us that we matter. You might feel like you don't have any friends now but that doesn't mean you won't have any in the future. There may even be someone already waiting to be your friend.

Female friendships

In books, films and music, female friendships are given a bad rap – full of gossiping, jealousy and competing for dates. But this is such a tired and false idea. Society puts so much emphasis on romantic relationships and ignores the beauty and strength in female friendships.

JOURNAL TIME

1. Draw your friendship circle

Come up with an avatar or doodle of yourself and your closest friends.

> "My friends are my backbone, I can always count on them to be there for me."
> Jemima (15)

Friendship labels

Did you know that there are different levels of friendship?

If you hang around in a large group, it might be tempting to think EVERYONE is your friend. But if you pay attention, there are some people in the group who you really connect with and others not so much. Understanding friendship labels can be helpful in shaping your expectations of people.

Best or close friends

These are the people whose friendship matters most – you can confide in them about anything and everything. Some people might have one best friend; others might have a handful of close friends. They are going through the THICK of it with you.

Acquaintances

An acquaintance is someone you know or see around who has not become a proper friend. You might say hello to them but that's as far as it goes.

Group friends

These people share a friendship circle with you. They are fun to hang out with but you probably won't call them when you're upset. You hang with them when you're in the mood to socialise, have a laugh and a good time.

"They're really good fun, I am always laughing around them."
Izzy (13)

"My friends have made the story of my life. In a thousand ways they have turned my limitations into beautiful privileges."
Helen Keller

2. What do friendships mean to you?

Have a think about why you love doing life with your best friends. Take a moment to write some of these reasons down as a little bit of encouragement for difficult times.

Choosing friends

With adolescence comes more independence and the ability to CHOOSE who your friends are. But have you ever thought about why certain friends are in your life? It might be helpful to keep this phrase in mind:

"You are the company you keep."

I know. You have probably heard this statement a hundred times but it is true. The people you hang out with can influence your behaviour and there are loads of studies to show how powerful this can be.

One of my closest friends growing up used to complain a lot and talk about other people. I noticed that whenever I spent time with her, I would complain too and just feel down and cynical about the world; her attitude really affected me. I have since built friendships with confident, kind and ambitious women, and this has spurred me on to believe in myself and my abilities. Choose friends who inspire you and motivate you to be better.

> "If you want friends, be a friend. If you want good friends, be a good friend."
> Anonymous

Friends with similar values

There's nothing more draining than pretending to be someone you are not just to keep a friend around. Earlier on, we discussed the values, morals and beliefs that matter to us. This knowledge is powerful – if someone criticises you for your beliefs or way of life, they probably aren't a good friend. Surround yourself with people who share or respect and accept your values.

They make me laugh.

They respect my beliefs and choices.

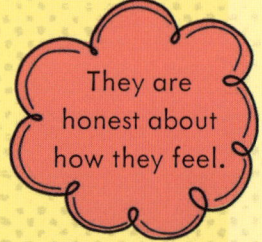

They are honest about how they feel.

Activity time
My best friend . . .

If you have a best or close friend, think about what makes them so amazing. Share this with your bestie, then ask them to say what it's like to be your friend. Check out the examples in the bubbles.

Are you a good friend?

Being a good friend does not mean being a perfect person – no one is perfect. But friends should make us feel positive about ourselves and our future. It is important that you reflect on whether you match up to the friendship standards you set for everyone else. Here are some of the attributes of a good friend.

Accepts
They recognise that we are all different and embrace what makes their friends unique.

Cares
They create the space for you to let your guard down and be vulnerable. They show they care for you in your weakest moments.

Celebrates
They big up the people around them. They don't compete with their friends or feel intimidated by their wins.

Apologises
We all have bad days and don't always say the right thing. A good friend will apologise when they get things wrong.

Shine theory

Two incredible women – Aminatou Sow and Ann Friedman – came up with 'shine theory', which states that if we pour our best selves into our friendships, we can become allies and not competitors.

A good friend knows that helping someone else's light to shine brightly will not diminish their own light but instead reflect it.

JOURNAL TIME

Create your 'friendworthy' wish list

List all the things that would make someone a good friend to you and you to them.

Friendship fallouts

It is inevitable; even the best of buds will clash. Falling out with a friend is totally normal. No matter how much you adore them or have in common, there will be areas of conflict and disagreement and that's okay. Fallouts do not have to mean a friendship has failed; in fact, having healthy conflict and disagreements with your friends can actually strengthen your relationships.

If you had a big argument or feel really hurt, you will need to ask yourself a few questions. Is this friendship worth saving? Are you prepared to make up with them if they don't make the move? Being the first to say sorry is difficult. It takes bravery and maturity because there is that stomach-turning fear that your friend could dismiss your apology. If this happens, stay calm. If you need to, you can walk away with closure and dignity knowing that you tried to make amends.

"My friend and I had a horrible argument; now she ignores me every time we see each other and we just don't talk anymore."
Leila (12)

Frenemies and toxic friends

Friendships, just like romantic relationships, can turn toxic and harmful or become damaging. We sometimes choose to be friends with people who we know aren't really there for us. When things are going well they are great, but when things are bad they can go cold on us until the cycle repeats itself and we see their good side again.

Who are they?

Frenemies are people who were kinda-sorta your friends once. On the surface, they appear to be your friends but they do not support you. It might be that they try to have 'one up' on you all the time, and you may feel uncomfortable sharing your success with them. The very worst kind of frenemy puts you down, lets you down and tries to keep you down there in the dumps.

Activity time
Toxic friendships

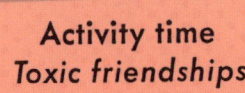

Unsure whether it's a toxic friendship? Ask yourself these questions:

- When you don't want to join in, do they make fun of you?
- Does it feel like the end of the world if you don't do what your friend says?
- After putting you down, do they make you doubt yourself by saying it was all a joke?
- Do you sometimes feel forced to do things you're uncomfortable with to fit in?

Story time

I attended three different primary schools, so I had to go through the cycle of making new friends and leaving them again multiple times. It was really difficult. At the last primary school I went to, I joined in Year Six. I was quite nervous, but I felt this school would be different because I already knew someone – I'll call her Bisi. She went to my church and we were on quite friendly terms, or so I thought . . .

Before starting, I visited the school to meet the teachers and students. Bisi made quite a big show of us knowing each other and that made me feel happy. That summer, I actually started to look forward to starting at this new school, so imagine my shock when September came and everyone ignored me. I thought at first that maybe they were just shy but it was more than that.

Bisi smiled at me occasionally but kept her distance. For the first few months, I spent break and lunch alone and was completely perplexed. After Christmas, the teachers announced a residential trip. Initially, I did not want to go – I literally had no friends – but my parents weren't having it.

Bisi was not on this trip and I finally realised why everyone had been ignoring me. Bisi had told them that I was rude and two-faced, and because we knew each other from church, they all believed her. However, without Bisi around, the class got to see me for who I really was and make their own decisions about me. Let's just say that their perception of me changed, and Bisi revealed herself as an unreliable person and a frenemy indeed.

REFLECTION

There are many reasons why Bisi may have chosen to behave this way — insecurity, jealousy or home-life problems. While we can recognise that people may be having difficulties, this should never excuse or normalise harmful behaviour. We all have unfavourable qualities or weaknesses, but that does not make it okay to cause others to feel hurt, shame or fear.

Peer pressure

Peer pressure is real, and wanting to fit in can mean we push our boundaries to keep friendships going. If toxic friends put pressure on you, it can be hard to stand up to them. There are also times when you might put pressure on yourself to please them.

Maybe there's a group of people that you really want to chill with, but they are doing something that is completely out of your comfort zone. You might worry that walking away or saying no risks the group seeing you as odd or babyish, so instead you put pressure on yourself to conform, thinking that maybe they will like you better. But there's no guarantee they will. Be brave; let the group know what you believe. It's not easy, but your safety and peace of mind is the most important thing.

> "Sometimes it just feels easier to go along with what my friends are doing, even though it makes me feel really bad afterwards."
> *Kiran (13)*

Activity time
Toxic group

Questions to ask yourself when you feel under pressure from people:

- Do I actually fit into this group?
- Do I want to be a part of this group?
- Why does being a part of it mean this much to me?

When friendships change

As you go through changes in life, your friendship circle will begin to look a bit different. Starting secondary school or moving house sometimes means leaving old friends behind, which can feel daunting. But your best friends don't have to disappear just because you're not at the same school. In some cases, you might mature quicker than your friends or vice versa. Growing apart and having different interests does not have to mean that the friendship is over, but it can present a natural opportunity to ask yourself if you still want this person in your life.

"My best friend is a boy; he always gives me jokes and is so easy to talk to. It's annoying how everyone thinks we like each other though. I think it's been getting to him because we don't talk as much any more."
Bolu (10)

"The thought of no longer knowing the friends I grew up with is so scary. It'll be like losing a part of my childhood."
Miriam (13)

"We used to be so close in primary school – now it's awkward any time I see her."
Stacey (13)

JOURNAL TIME
Changing friendships

Write about any changes you have noticed in your friendships and how they make you feel.

Friendship breakups

A friendship breakup happens when either you or someone else decides that your friendship has run its course and it is time to move on. It might involve confronting a frenemy and telling them how their behaviour makes you feel. This could allow them to acknowledge the pain they are causing, apologise and change for the better. However, it is important to know that some frenemies will not change. Be prepared to let those people go.

> "You can't make homes out of human beings; someone should have already told you that."
> Warsan Shire

The truth is no one is guaranteed to stay in your life forever. Following a friendship breakup, a part of your grieving process will be finding the joy in doing things for yourself and by yourself. Think about some activities you could do to enjoy your own company.

JOURNAL TIME
Write a friendship breakup letter

Is there someone you need to be honest with? Include all your thoughts and feelings in the letter. Name the wrongs and issues you encountered. Be honest and open. No one is going to read this letter, so don't hold back. Once you've written it, you can choose either to rip it up into a million little pieces or bury it. This could help release any anger and bitterness you might be feeling.

Friendship matters

In order to navigate this world bravely, you need a community of people who have got your back. Friends matter, and who you choose to surround yourself with is not a decision to take lightly. It is important to celebrate the power of female friendships and reject the myth that girls cannot get along. That said, friendships can be complicated. Understanding the different levels of friendships can empower you to set healthy boundaries with people and understand the role they play in your life. It is normal for friends to drift apart or even fall out, but they can come back together and rebuild trust. Your friendships will change as you evolve; there might be bumps and breakups along the way, but do not let that discourage you from opening up to new people. There is an anonymous saying that I firmly believe in:

"You still have not met all the people who are going to love you."

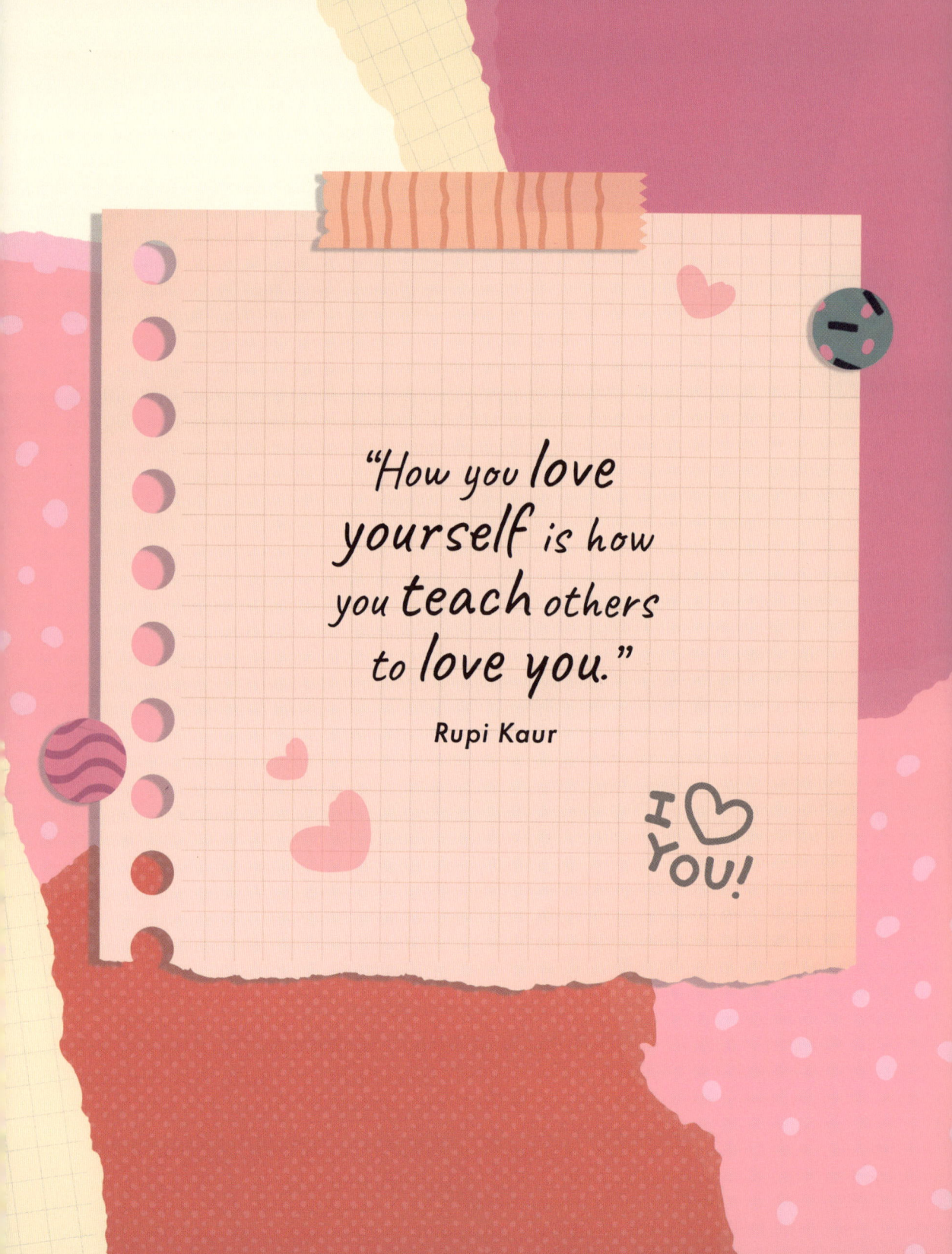

Chapter 4
Relationships and Self-love

Let's explore . . . confidence, self-care, love, relationships and the power of consent.

In this part of the book, we will focus on how to have a healthy relationship with yourself and then explore what a healthy relationship with another person should look like.

No one is an island. Although at times you might find yourself alone (and maybe even prefer it that way), you are part of a whole — whether that's your family, a friendship circle, a school, a club or religious community. Human connection is a deep bond that's formed between groups of people. Socialising can improve your life by lowering anxiety, regulating emotions, building self-esteem and helping you feel empathy.

"Talk to yourself like someone you love."
Brené Brown

Connecting with yourself

The most important relationship is the one you have with yourself. Sometimes we get so busy being the bestest best friend, loving our siblings, helping out at home or caring for our furry friends that we don't connect with ourselves. Do you generously share your love with others but forget to show that kindness, care and attention to yourself? In Chapter 1, we looked at identity – getting to know yourself. But you can't stop there; to know yourself is to love yourself.

Here are some signs that you are disconnected from yourself and need to up your dose of self-love and self-care.

- Having a harsh inner voice

- Struggling to have a positive self-image

- Not feeling confident in your abilities

- Negative thoughts and feelings about yourself

"I am always trying to overperform and please my parents but it never feels enough."
Grace (15)

"All the girls are prettier than me. I just look hideous."
Marie (13)

"I don't matter and everyone thinks so too. I wish I was someone different."
Shola (12)

Self-love, self-care and **self-esteem** are major buzzwords. Let's take a moment to define them and look at each in turn.

Self-esteem: The confidence and value you have in your worth and abilities.

Self-love: Loving, accepting and appreciating yourself.

Self-care: The practical actions you take to show yourself love and look after your mental, emotional and physical wellbeing.

Your self-esteem

You could have low self-esteem for a range of reasons. Maybe you have always felt negatively about yourself, or perhaps you're going through something that has changed the way you feel about your value. It could be that you only occasionally feel negatively about yourself when triggered by a situation – like getting a bad grade or being picked last for teams in PE.

The tricky thing about having low self-esteem is that it's not always obvious because we often wear a mask to hide our insecurity. It can be painful, and even embarrassing, to admit that we have issues with confidence. But this book is all about being brave and learning to live authentically because **you matter.**

Activity time: *Get creative!*

It can sometimes feel like we only get to be creative when we have positive and affirming things to say about ourselves, but art is not always happy. Being creative can help release tension, frustration and pain.

Pick one of these methods to showcase how you think and feel about yourself:

- Write a poem or spoken word piece
- Mindmap ideas for a short film
- Draw a picture
- Write a journal entry
- Come up with a rap or song
- Take a photo

JOURNAL TIME
Acknowledge the issues

Think about yourself and your abilities, then write down all the emotions and words that come up.
For instance:
Pride, shame, joy, enough, jealousy, guilt, stress, control, confusion, doubt, confidence, fear, sadness, hope, tension, awe, disapproval, gratitude, rejection, acceptance.

How often do you believe in yourself?
1. A lot of the time
2. Occasionally
3. Rarely
4. Never

Do you worry about what other people think of you?
1. A lot of the time
2. Occasionally
3. Rarely
4. Never

Write down any of the below situations that make you doubt yourself:
- Speaking in front of others
- Making new friends
- Asking for help
- Asking questions
- Being sporty or active
- Learning something new
- Saying no
- Standing up for your rights
- Telling someone they've hurt you
- Doing creative things

Include any other situations that make you feel doubtful.

Take time to reflect on your responses. This task is to help you acknowledge any issues and give you the words to describe how you're feeling. If your answers show that you have issues with your esteem, it might be a good idea to show this page to a friend, mentor, teacher or adult you trust and talk it through. I know it's a scary thing to share, but being brave and honest with people can help you to connect and feel less alone.

Story time

Remember that I mentioned two of my strengths are being analytical and a strong communicator? Yes, well I was always quite 'good' at school. While I celebrated the fact that I did well, I did not realise that I was basing the whole sum of my identity and value on the shaky foundation of being 'the smart one'. I constantly felt under pressure to show just how capable I was, how hard-working, how talented. It drained me and made me anxious – feeling like I constantly had something to prove. So, as you can imagine, when I had the biggest flop of my academic life during my A-levels, I ended up completely hating myself.

I did not get the triple A* grades I was predicted. I did not get into my first or second choice of university. I was anxious, burnt out and no longer 'the smart one'. It felt like I had failed not just at my A-levels, but in my identity. For the longest time, I felt like I had nothing to offer because nothing of worth remained in me. I had to go on a journey of many years to challenge that harmful and destructive belief. I learned to develop a more balanced, grounded view of my identity and discovered that who

TAKE TIME TO LOVE YOURSELF FOR WHO YOU ARE.

I am is more than what I do and how well I do it.

It's important to remember that while it feels good to be celebrated and acknowledged for your strengths, it can be harmful to establish your sense of worth and self-esteem purely in your accomplishments. It's a shaky foundation.

You are valuable because you are human, a being of great dignity.

You have a heart, mind, body and soul. The great things you do – your strengths and talents – should be celebrated; you absolutely deserve your flowers! But what if you do not achieve those things? Will you still matter to you? Know that being yourself is sufficient and take time to love yourself for who you are, not just for what you do, create or produce.

REFLECTION

What would you say your strengths and talents are?

Is there one part of your identity that you feel defines you?

How would you cope if this definition stopped being true?

Let's build that esteem!

It is empowering to know that self-esteem can be built up. You might find talking about low self-esteem easier than speaking up about what positive self-esteem would look like, but let's go into unchartered waters!

What would having positive self-esteem look like for you?

> Understanding that I don't have to be perfect to be loved.

> Being confident about what I can do.

> Loving myself without conditions.

> Putting my wellbeing first.

> Staying true to my values.

> Knowing that the real me is good enough.

It may feel like a big challenge to change the way you see, think and feel about yourself. But take a moment to allow your mind to wander and visualise the best version of you. Who is this person? What do they like? What will they accept? What won't they settle for? How do they feel about themselves, their abilities and their future?

JOURNAL TIME

Write a letter to your highest self

Dear Highest Self . . .

You can use the above questions if you need prompts. Include in your letter a promise to show up as your highest self every day, whether in big or small ways.

Nurturing yourself

Self-love and self-care are talked about so much, especially online. Self-love doesn't have to be this fairy-tale place where we adore every single thing about ourselves. Some days will be easier than others, and loving yourself means committing to sticking through the tough days and granting yourself compassion instead of criticism.

If your best friend was having a bad day, would you tell them to get over it or support them? Chances are you would show your friend that they are loved and cared for. Isn't it silly then that we struggle to show this kindness to ourselves? Self-love means understanding that some days may be difficult and you might need some extra TLC (tender loving care).

Learn to challenge your inner critic because the more you listen to that voice, the more you give it power.

> "Once I learned to like me more than others did, then I didn't have to worry about being the funniest, or the most popular or the prettiest. I was the best me and I only ever tried to be that."
> Issa Rae

Activity time: *Take the 'Rosenberg Self-esteem Scale' questionnaire*
It is used globally by young people, adults, therapists and doctors worldwide to assess self-esteem.
Visit **wwnorton.com/college/psych/psychsci/media/rosenberg.htm** to complete it.

Self-care

You may have heard about popular self-care tips, like writing down affirmations every morning or the 'THAT GIRL' morning routine, where caring for yourself has certain aesthetics and guidelines . . . It looks like having a tall glass of blended celery, kale and broccoli, then going on a ten-mile run, followed by a ten-step facial routine and lighting lavender-scented candles, all before school! But truly showing yourself care and love means more than gulping down green juice each morning or running yourself rose-scented bubble baths every night. While some people might find these activities calming and relaxing (more power to them), it's important to know that connecting with yourself and building your esteem through self-care doesn't need to live up to someone else's standard or hashtag. These trends encourage comparisons and can leave us feeling like we're not doing enough for ourselves. Personally, if I make self-care about doing all these pretty things, I end up feeling even WORSE when I inevitably fail to follow through with it all.

> "Caring for myself is not self-indulgence, it is self-preservation, and that is an act of political warfare."
> Audre Lorde

REFLECTION

Think of some authentic self-care practices. Don't worry about the tips that are popular right now or what everyone else is doing. You might prefer a herbal tea to green juice, or maybe you loathe running and would rather dance in your bedroom. What will make YOU feel loved, cared for and nourished?

Self-respect

Having a healthy connection and relationship with yourself means having self-respect and honouring your boundaries (the limit of what you consider acceptable behaviour). You may find that you don't have a problem respecting other people's wishes but allow yours to be trampled on to please everyone. Having our boundaries crossed can crush our self-esteem and leave us feeling burnt out or violated. Respecting yourself means that you think you are worthy and deserving. This sets the standard for others too – learn not to give your time and energy to people who make you feel unworthy, sad or doubtful.

Be your own bestie

Setting boundaries is not easy and communicating them can be uncomfortable and challenging. There are many legit fears – what if my friends say I've changed? What if I'm called weird? It takes bravery to stand up for yourself, but it's better to feel internally safe and secure than be surrounded by people who don't respect you. Becoming your own best friend is not about being unpopular. It's the path taken by those with strong minds and standards – people who understand the power of friendship but will not depend on others for their happiness.

Learning to enjoy being in your own company means you can be choosy about who gets to come into your life. Being your own bestie looks like being proud of yourself, learning to trust yourself and honouring your instincts.

> "How you love yourself is how you teach others to love you."
> *Rupi Kaur*

Activity time
Make your 'alone' feel good

Make a list of all the things that make you feel happy. This will be personal to you but here are some suggestions:

Read – Listen to an audiobook – Dance – Write a story – Take pictures of beautiful things – Discover new places – Go for a walk – Give yourself a facial – Paint your nails – Create a playlist with your favourite tunes – Try making a TikTok recipe

If you're not ready to do these things by yourself, for yourself, have a think about activities you would like to feel comfortable doing alone – these are goals you can work towards!

Let's talk love

Love is your greatest ally. Whether you're loving yourself, another person or your pet rabbit, love is a source of infinite strength. So let's talk loving other people – especially romantically. Do you like or love or maybe even have a crush on someone? Have you ever in the past? Maybe you're reading this and thinking, "Ew, I would much rather chew my toenails than even think about having a crush." That is completely fine! You can skip the next few pages if you're not ready to get into this topic just yet (or ever). But for those of you who have skimmed through the book looking for this exact section and are thinking, "FINALLY!" – let's go there!

During puberty, massive changes are happening in your body and mind. It is such a monumental time because it's part of your transition from childhood to adulthood. If your biological sex is female, you may find that your breasts are beginning to develop and just wearing a vest is not enough any more. There may be other changes too, like seeing hair on your vulva or armpits, and you might find that you need products you've never had to use before, like deodorant. These physical changes are caused by the active hormones coursing through your body, which also change how your brain thinks and the way you feel.

With puberty comes a new range of intense feelings, such as having a crush, feeling attracted to someone or wondering what it would be like to kiss or fall in love. Remember that people experience these feelings at different times, so no rush or pressure if you're not there. If you are feeling worried about puberty, take a look at the Childline website for more information on how to cope with this immense change.

Some grown-ups might feel as though you are too young to learn about romantic relationships but that's not true. Understanding healthy relationships, consent and personal boundaries should happen way before you agree to be with someone.

Sexuality

Your sexuality is all about who you feel attracted to, either physically or emotionally. Everyone is different; there is no right or wrong way to feel. You may have thought a lot about your sexuality or you may not feel ready to address it yet. Many young people take a while to work it out and there is no rush to define yourself. If you're struggling with your feelings around sexuality, you can get support. Take a look at the resources section at the end of the book for advice.

That first crush

A crush is when you're drawn to another person who gives you butterflies and might make you feel tongue-tied or nervous. Crushes tend to be the starting point for feelings that can develop with time – you might find that there is a growing desire to hold hands, cuddle or even kiss another person. A crush doesn't have to be someone you know in real life. When I was growing up, my friends and I had sooo many celebrity crushes – it was exhausting! Crushes can feel overwhelming but don't forget that they are often based on an exaggerated, fantasy version of the person.

From crush to relationships

While this is probably unlikely if you have a crush on Harry Styles or Halle Bailey, if you have a crush on someone in real life and around your age, chances are you might be curious about whether a relationship could work. However, there is no need to rush. Enjoy being you, falling in love with yourself and being loved by friends and family. In the years to come, you'll have many opportunities to date, maybe get your heart broken and probably break a few hearts yourself! Everything's a process. Take your time and never feel pressured into being in a relationship if you don't want one.

Healthy relationships

If you are in a relationship, it's important to ask yourself if it feels healthy or unhealthy. Early on, it can be easy to miss red flags because you are being swept off your feet. Every relationship looks different, but there are some common traits in healthy ones.

Trust allows you to be open and forgiving. It means you can rely on your partner. If there is no trust, a relationship is likely to be chaotic and controlled by negative feelings like jealousy.

Honesty is about being truthful with your partner and them with you. It is closely linked to trust because if your partner tells a lie, you are less likely to trust them.

Kindness is about looking out for your partner, affirming them and lifting them up with words and actions.

Fairness is having an equal say. If there is no fairness, the relationship will start to feel like a power struggle with one person dominating the other.

Respect looks like recognising the boundaries another person has and not pushing past or undermining them.

Support means helping your partner to shine brightly and never feel alone. You are happy for them when they succeed, not intimidated.

Physical feelings

As you go through puberty, your body is undergoing a whole new experience. You might not believe this, but you have 7 trillion nerve endings inside you! They allow you to experience physical touch and all the emotions that come with it – like the feel of a gentle breeze on your skin or the softness of a fluffy pillow. So many parts of your body have been designed to feel good when touched and there's no shame in that.

With puberty will come new and intense emotional and physical feelings. They can be triggered by different situations, like watching a romantic movie or fantasising about a crush. But sometimes you can feel 'turned on' for simply no reason at all – puberty gets like that! Talking about sexual arousal often feels taboo, but it shouldn't because it's a natural physical response. Although these new feelings can take you by surprise, there is no need to feel shame. You can navigate them in a way that is empowering, safe and healthy for you and other people.

Porn

Porn is sexually explicit videos and pictures created by actors. Often, porn films and content will have been made in unsafe or uncomfortable conditions. Porn can be dangerous because it can normalise behaviour that is harmful or violent in real life. Watching it can feel exciting, but porn can be damaging to your perspective on sex and give a false impression of how real people behave in a healthy sexual relationship. Porn can also breed insecurity by warping our ideas of what bodies look like.

> ⚠️ If you've seen or been shown something that made you feel uncomfortable, remember that you can always talk to a trusted adult about it.

Consent

Giving consent (permission for something to happen) is essential for keeping healthy boundaries. The ability to touch and feel can be a beautiful part of the human experience and it's one of the ways we connect with people. It could be a hug, a high-five or a knowing hand squeeze. Physical touch is also an area that so many people get wrong and where boundaries are crossed.

Sex, consent and the law

Sexual intercourse can happen when two consenting adults want to express love, feel close to each other or make a baby. In the UK, there is an age of consent; this is a recognised age where you can legally consent to having sex. In the UK it is 16 and in Ireland it is 17. According to law, sex is not just about penetration (when a penis enters a vagina or anus). Sex also includes anything being put inside the vagina or anus and any sexual contact with the mouth.

Anyone underage who engages in sexual activity is breaking the law. Any person older than the age of consent who sexually engages with someone underage also breaks the law. These laws are here to protect children from sexual exploitation. If anyone under 13 is engaged in sexual activity, they would be seen as victims of child abuse, not as law breakers.

Some young people under the age of 16 engage in 'agreed' sexual activity. Although this is illegal, the law is not put in place with the aim of criminalising this behaviour. If you are under 16 and you need to access services for contraception, sexual health or pregnancy advice, you will not be criminalised and you'll be able to obtain this support confidentially.

⚠️ Although lots of talk about sex may be going around your school and it can feel like 'everyone is doing it', statistics show that many young people don't have sex until they are in their twenties.

Be the boss of your body

Your body is your space, your temple, your home and sanctuary. EVERYBODY, regardless of their gender, race, ethnicity, height, disability, weight or shape, has the right to autonomy (making their own decisions) over their bodies. People, particularly girls and women, are often policed on what they can or can't do with their bodies or how loud or quiet their voices should be.

> "Love yourself enough to set boundaries... You teach people how to treat you by deciding what you will and won't accept."
> — Anna Taylor

Boundaries

Boundaries are a way of setting limits with other people and yourself. Boundaries can be physical but also personal, emotional, ethical and mental. It is super important for the people you connect with to know which boundaries they cannot cross. For example, as you get older, certain types of physical touching may no longer sit right with you.

Unwanted touching does not always come from people who intend to bring you harm, but that doesn't take away from the fact that it is unwelcome. You can still tell these people to stop. You might find this difficult at first, but you can say things like, "Please don't touch me," or "I would like some space," or even ask, "What are you doing?" to get them to reflect on how their behaviour is impacting you. Remember, your voice is your power.

What if I change my mind?

As you know from the chapter on identity, we are constantly changing our minds and choosing better for ourselves. You are allowed to change your mind about your boundaries too! It is totally okay if you no longer feel comfortable doing something that was previously fine. The situation is different and maybe you're different too; everyone must respect that.

JOURNAL TIME: Know your boundaries

Take the time to think about what your boundaries are. Ponder some of the examples below and come up with your own.

Physical boundaries
- Don't burst into my room without knocking first
- Don't borrow my clothes without asking
- I only hug friends and family that I know
- I don't want to be seen naked

Emotional boundaries
- I refuse to take the blame for someone else's mistakes
- I expect respect and kindness
- I will ask for space when I need it

Moral boundaries
- I won't make fun of people who are different to me
- Don't use racist or homophobic language around me
- I won't steal from others

Power dynamics

There are many reasons why communicating your boundaries can be challenging, especially when the issues of power and authority come into the mix. Power is about having influence or control. It is not always bad; in fact it can be used as a force for good – for example, a celebrity using their platform to raise awareness of a positive cause. However, power imbalances can make it difficult to give consent. Sometimes, a person might struggle to say no because they feel like they don't have the power to be heard.

"No is a complete sentence."
Anonymous

Power imbalances sometimes happen because the other person is physically bigger or stronger. A difference in age and status could also make a young person feel intimidated and unable to say no due to a fear of being punished or missing out on an opportunity; but remember, your voice counts too – feel empowered to communicate that your rights need to be respected.

Activity time
Power in relationships

Browse this list of relationships with power dynamics. Can you think of any more?

- Youth leader and young person
- Teacher and student
- Celebrity and fan
- Influencer and follower
- Religious leader and worshipper
- Doctor and patient
- Police officer and citizen
- Add your own . . .

REFLECTION

Here are some ways to challenge a power imbalance:

- **Call it out.**
- **Check in with yourself.** How are you feeling? Scared or confused?
- **Walk away** or take a break from the situation.
- Can you think of another way to challenge the imbalance?

Reminders about love

We have talked about the things that can sometimes go wrong in relationships when boundaries are crossed and differences are not respected. But it is important to remember that healthy and beautiful relationships and friendships do exist. Here are a few points and reminders about love to keep in mind going forwards. It might seem like there should be NO rules when it comes to love because of all the intense emotions involved, but rules and boundaries help protect us and our hearts. Here are some reminders to keep in mind as you grow and find yourself exploring romantic love. I'll start you off with a few, but the goal is that you reflect on this chapter and write a few love reminders for yourself.

No one gets to control who you love

YOUR CHOICE matters when it comes to love. Absolutely no one should get to control who you like or date. This might be a friend who 'dares you' or pressures you to say yes when someone asks you out, or a pestering auntie with cultural expectations pushing you to date someone you don't like or even arranging a relationship without your consent.

> "My dad has told me that he is arranging a marriage between me and a boy in our community when I turn 16. I don't want this, but I am scared to reject their arrangement."
>
> Aisha (15)

This level of pressure is immense, wrong and in some cases illegal. You must speak to a trusted adult if you are ever feeling forced to be in a relationship.

Never ignore the warning signs

Warning signs are often referred to as 'red flags'. They could include things like anger management issues, jealousy, gaslighting or someone constantly putting you down. It can be super tempting to ignore the red flags, get swept up in the emotions of the moment and just hope for the best, but you deserve to feel respected, safe and supported. For more on toxic relationships, see p189.

Consent is power

Anyone who tries to refuse your lack of consent can be left alone. Consent acknowledges your freedom and independence. It also helps to build trusting relationships with others because it prevents them from misunderstanding you. When consent is communicated and respected between two people, they can honour and protect each other's boundaries.

JOURNAL TIME

Write your own love reminders

Come up with at least two more love reminders for yourself.

Take back your power

The most important relationship is the one you have with yourself. That's why this chapter first focused on self-love, self-esteem and having a healthy connection with yourself. When you love and accept who you are, the people around you will see this, admire you and respect you for it.

Girls are often made to think that they can't say no, that they have to be nice, polite and play the game of pleasing everyone. These outdated views do not serve us. Your voice is your power. Giving or refusing to give consent is how you protect yourself and your boundaries. Absolutely no one's company is worth it if they make you feel scared, unloved, uncomfortable or insecure.

Has anything you've read in this chapter challenged you or even spurred you into action? Why not get a group of friends together and have a conversation about it. If anything you've read has upset, triggered or concerned you, please seek out a trusted adult. For more information about the sensitive issues this chapter covers, you can turn to the resource section at the back of this book.

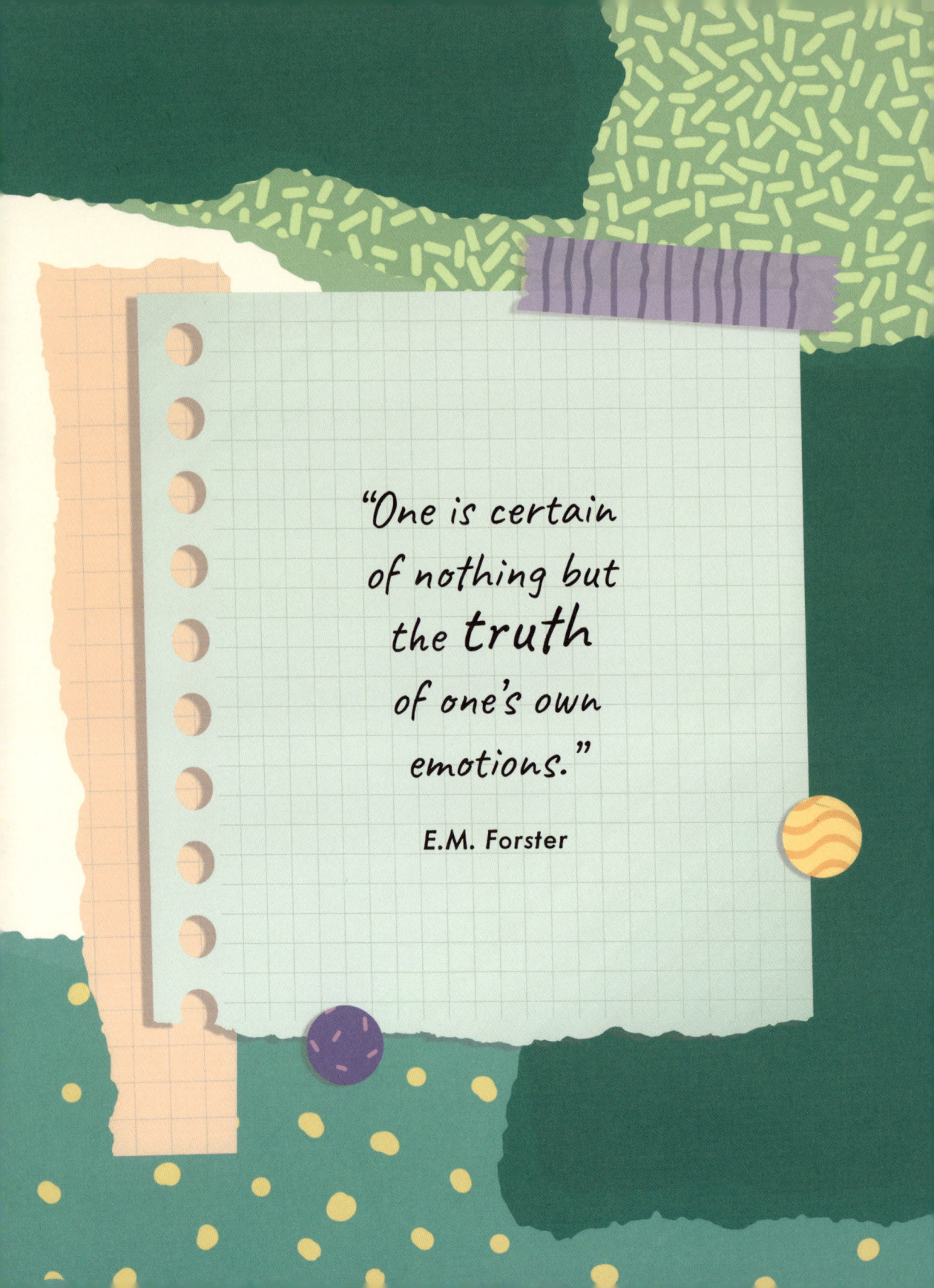

Chapter 5
Mind, Mood and Feelings

Let's explore . . . your brain, emotions, how to fail, looking after your mental health and the power of sleep.

Your brain

There was a time in history when the brain was pretty much disregarded. The ancient Egyptians thought it much less important than the heart and would pull it out of dead pharaohs through their noses! Aristotle, an ancient Greek philosopher, thought the brain's main function was to cool down the heart. Philosophers in the Middle Ages got closer to the truth, believing it had three areas that housed the imagination, memory and reasoning. With amazing developments in science and technology, we can now see detailed scans of the brain, which help us to map its activity and understand it better. Your brain is INCREDIBLE. It can fit into the palm of your hand, yet it has more cells in it than there are people on the planet!

Neuroscientists have found that the brain is neuroplastic; this means it stretches and grows in the same way you have over the years. Changes in the adolescent brain start at about 11 years old, and up to the age of 20 it is developing a whole lot. It has an incredible ability to learn, adapt and respond to new experiences. The more you explore your brain, the better you get at understanding your thoughts, feelings and yourself.

Your hormones

Adolescence is a super hormonal time. This applies to young people of all genders, by the way; it's not just a 'period thing'. There are over 50 hormones in the human body, but dopamine, cortisol, serotonin and melatonin are the main four responsible for changes in your behaviour during puberty.

Hippocampus
This part of the brain has to do with memory. During puberty, it creates thousands more cells than in adulthood.

Prefrontal cortex
This part of the brain oversees all your decision-making. It is responsible for your ability to plan, prioritise, solve problems, control impulses and understand the consequences of your actions.

Amygdala
This is a small, almond-shaped region in the brain that helps regulate emotions, impulses, aggression and instinctive behaviour. While your prefrontal cortex is maturing, you will rely more on the amygdala.

Cortisol
Also known as the stress hormone, it is produced in your adrenal glands and becomes elevated when you experience anxiety or stress. That said, a certain amount of cortisol is healthy and normal. It peaks naturally in the morning so has an important function driving your 'get up and go' instinct.

Melatonin
A hormone produced in response to darkness. It helps with your internal clock so has a key role in your sleep-wake cycle. In teens, melatonin is released two hours later than in adults and children, which is why they often want to go to bed late and lie in!

Dopamine
The reward hormone that is responsible for you feeling satisfaction and motivation when you achieve something.

Serotonin
The feel-good hormone in your brain which regulates your mood. Low levels of serotonin have been linked to anxiety and depression.

Emotions

Emotions are a part of human nature. Babies and younger children express their emotions by crying or laughing. They can show their feelings but don't yet know how to name them. As you develop, you may become better at understanding your emotions and putting them into words. This way, emotions can help you understand yourself and help others to understand you.

As you already know, during adolescence your brain is changing a lot. On top of this, there are many social changes, which can make the teen years feel confusing and worrying. As a teenager, I remember having so many different emotions and feelings in just one hour, never mind one day! If you too sometimes feel moody, you have the amygdala to thank for that! Remember, it's the area of your brain that manages your emotions and it goes through major changes during your teen years. It will eventually settle (I promise), but it does take some time. Understanding your emotions and developing emotional awareness can be super empowering because it helps you talk about your feelings and accept them more easily.

Activity time: *Talk about feelings*

Robert Plutchik's wheel of emotions can be a helpful tool, especially when it comes to talking about how you feel, which may be challenging. If you're struggling, have a look at the wheel diagram and pick out a word that is close to what you are feeling.

Which **WORD** best describes how you're feeling?

Can you spot **JOY**?

Can you see that it's opposite is **SADNESS**?

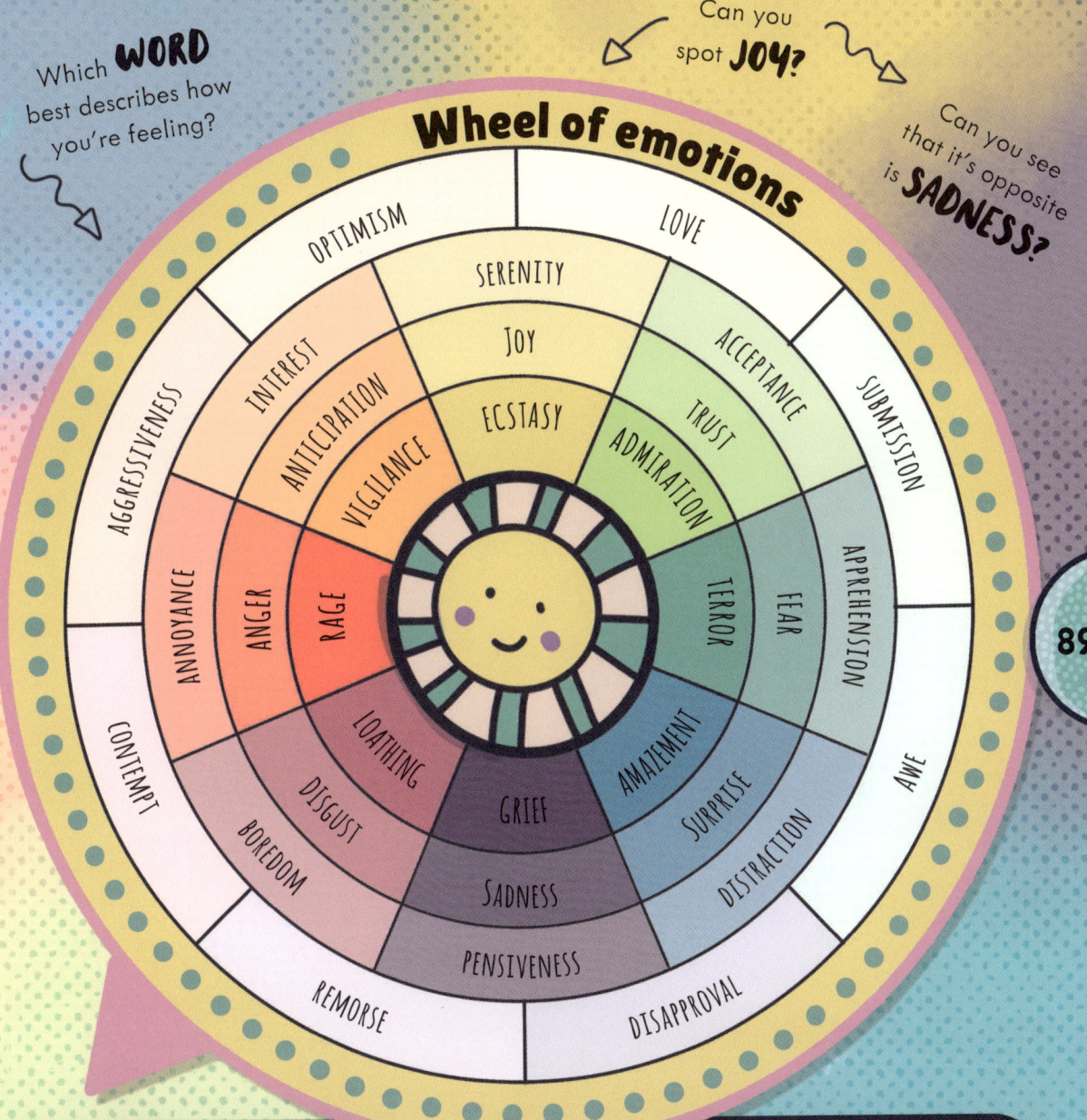

Wheel of emotions

89

According to psychologist Robert Plutchik, there are eight primary emotions: joy, trust, fear, surprise, sadness, anticipation, anger and disgust. By combining these, you experience more advanced emotions like love, disapproval, awe or aggressiveness. Plutchik created a 'wheel of emotions', which shows the relationships between each feeling.

Anger

Anger is an emotion we all experience from time to time but especially during adolescence. We can get angry for lots of reasons and feeling this emotion is completely normal.

> "I cannot **HIDE** my **ANGER** to spare you guilt, nor hurt feelings, nor answering anger; for to do so **INSULTS** and **TRIVIALIZES** all our efforts."
> — Audre Lorde

Feel the rage

Growing up, I was so conscious that Black girls were always portrayed as rude, sassy and loud. This stereotype was in the films I watched and books I read. So for a long time, I struggled to show when I was hurt and angry. I was afraid that by showing my emotions, I would become the 'angry Black woman' or the 'sassy Black girl' society expected me to be.

I think it is important for all girls to know that they are allowed to feel anger and other intense emotions that are not necessarily cute or pleasant. You do not have to suppress the anger or rage you are feeling and pretend to be totally fine if something or someone has hurt or upset you.

Listening to the stories of young people I was supporting in schools made me realise that anger is experienced in different ways.

Unlike my own experience, for some of these young people, anger is the only emotion they feel comfortable displaying. This might be because things are not great at home or they are being harassed and bullied, stressed by school or feel tired of carrying the responsibility for their younger siblings. Being unafraid to show strong emotions is important, but so is understanding the reasons behind your anger and taking back control over volatile feelings.

Being angry all the time can be harmful to you and the friendships and relationships that matter most.

TIPS FOR
taming the inner beast

Breathe deep and slow
Turn away from whatever or whoever triggered your anger and focus on regulating your breathing.

Use your words
Speaking to someone about your feelings is a great way to control them; just explain your thoughts. It could be a friend, a trusted adult or a helpline if you want to be anonymous. In the resources section at the back of the book, there is a list of organisations that are free to call, with trained people who are there to listen to you without judgement.

Blow off some steam
Anger produces a huge amount of energy within you and you may feel calmer once you release it. Run, power-walk, roar or even punch a pillow – find a safe way to use that fire.

Cool that temper
List five things that help you calm your anger.

Are you angry all the time without an obvious reason? It might be helpful to speak with a doctor, therapist or counsellor to get support.

"I want to be in CONTROL over how my RAGE is going to be used and I don't want it to be used against me because I refuse to confront it."
Brittney Cooper

You do not necessarily have control over your hormones, and the external factors that trigger anger may seem beyond your control. However, you can control how you react to anger and try to prevent it from becoming all-consuming. It can sometimes be easier to display rage than to admit that you're hurt or lonely or maybe even depressed.

Sadness

We all feel sad from time to time. No one is a bouncing ball of energy all day, every day. There are times we know exactly what has hurt us and there are other times we simply cannot figure out what has brought about our low mood and sadness.

Coping with sadness

Take time
You don't have to rush from sadness to happiness. Take the time to process what you are feeling. If you can, take time out from daily activities and prioritise looking after yourself. Revisit Chapter 4 and try some of the self-care practices and tools you've noted down.

Acknowledge the feels
You may understand the reason behind your sadness or you might not have a clue. Know that your feelings are valid and it's okay to not feel your best sometimes. There's no need to put on a false smile and keep up pretences; embrace what you are feeling.

Stay connected
Feeling sadness can make you want to withdraw into yourself but try not to give in to the impulse to hide. Social isolation and loneliness can worsen sadness. It might take all you've got but reach out – even if it's just by sending a text. A friendly voice, a listening ear or even someone cracking a joke might be just what you need.

Feeling sad sometimes is normal but if you're feeling low all the time, then you may need support for your mental health. More on this on p109.

Stress and anxiety

Stress and anxiety are linked and share many of the same symptoms but they are different. Stress is a response to an external cause, like struggling with schoolwork or going on a long flight, that goes away once the cause has been resolved. Anxiety is a normal human feeling of fear or panic that can be triggered by a stressful situation. Everybody feels anxious sometimes, but usually we calm down and feel better again once the worry has passed. However, some people experience persistent anxiety which is not caused by external factors or anxiety in response to 'normal', day-to-day activities. These types of anxiety may be medically diagnosed as a mental health condition. For more on anxiety, see p108.

Mental
- Feeling overwhelmed
- Constantly worrying
- Being forgetful
- Struggling to make decisions

Physical
- Chest pain or a faster heartbeat
- Headaches or dizziness
- Muscle tension or pain
- Stomach problems

Behavioural
- Being irritable and snappy
- Sleeping too much or too little
- Avoiding certain places or people
- Spending more time than usual in virtual worlds such as games or social media
- Focusing on what or how much you eat
- Self-harming

Stress symptoms

People often say they are stressed, but what does stress look and feel like? What are the signs? Some symptoms are obvious — maybe you're feeling nervous or panicked — but there are other symptoms that do not at first appear to be caused by stress, like headaches, migraines and tummy aches. It is important to speak to a trusted adult or doctor if you are experiencing any of the symptoms described on the left.

REFLECTION

What are your symptoms of stress?

Are you able to tell when you're feeling stressed?

How about if it's happening to your friend or a family member?

Managing stress

Stress is emotional tension or mental strain, and we feel it as a physical response to certain triggers. Being a young person in today's world is A LOT and many adults don't recognise how complicated your life can be. Even when you are minding your own business, it can feel like the world is falling apart. Whether it's global injustice, the climate crisis, family pressures or friendship issues, life is full of stressors.

Digital pressures

Cue the influencers, trends, follower counts, likes and, of course, the filters. There is so much pressure to conform to unreal beauty and lifestyle standards and to be phenomenal and impressive all the time. For more on the highs and lows of digital culture, check out Chapter 8.

Physical and hormonal changes

When our bodies change as puberty takes hold, this can trigger a whole load of uncertainty and insecurity.

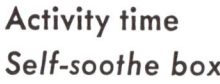

Activity time
Self-soothe box

Whenever you are feeling anxious or stressed, you can reach for a self-soothe box filled with sensory items you can smell, touch, taste or focus on. The box can be big and have a permanent spot in your room or it could be a small travel-sized box that you can use when you are on the go. Have a look at some of the items on the right, pick out your favourites and get inspiration for your own self-soothe box.

Smell
Some scents, such as lavender or peppermint, bring relief from anxiety and stress by calming the brain.

Choose your favourite scent – it could be a candle, room spray or essential oil.

Touch
A great way to distract your hands, relax your muscles and relieve some stress.

Playdough

Stress balls

Fidget cubes

Sound
Pick sounds that help calm you. They could be upbeat to lift your mood or slow in tempo to help quieten your mind.

Wind-up music box

Calming sounds such as rainfall or white noise

Playlist of songs

Other items
Bottle of water for hydration

Affirmation cards and quotes

Breathing cards (shapes that you trace with directions for breathing)

Self-soothe box

Fight, flight, fawn or freeze

Stressful situations can trigger us into fight, flight, fawn or freeze mode. These responses are how our bodies react when we are threatened with a dangerous or difficult situation. Our hearts beat faster, our hands and feet go cold or clammy and we might even get an upset stomach. These symptoms come from our brains triggering the release of chemicals – adrenaline and cortisol – to prompt our bodies to respond to the danger quickly. This was vital for the survival of early humans who needed to escape wild animals and it still has its uses; adrenaline surges can help us deal with crisis situations. However, it's a problem if our fight, flight, fawn or freeze response is being triggered constantly or by day-to-day things.

An excess of cortisol can negatively impact your health, mood and thoughts. When some people are overloaded with stress, it can lead to aggression, anxiety, physical illness or other unhealthy behaviours, like eating disorders and self-harm, as a control or coping mechanism. If you're suffering with stress, turn to p108 for help.

Tame stress

Experiencing calm and pleasure in your life should not be a luxury; they are necessities that you deserve. No one is designed to run on stress mode perpetually. It may help to accept the humbling truth that you cannot control every aspect of your life and it is not the end of the world if things don't pan out exactly how you expect. You may not be able to totally eliminate the triggers for stress, anxiety and fear, but take an active role in ensuring you have plenty of time for relaxation to balance things out. There are techniques and practices you can take up to make you feel more grounded and at peace within yourself.

What you can do when feeling anxious about a stressful situation:

- Make a list of the things that make you feel anxious. This will help you to face your worries and feel more in control of them.
- Grab some pencils and draw something or use a colouring book.
- Regularly move your body or do your favourite exercise.
- Speak to someone about what is worrying you.
- Look at something beautiful in nature. Allow it to ground you in the here and now.
- Reach for your self-soothe box.
- Breathe in and out deeply and slowly or try 4-4-8 breathing, where you breathe in for four, hold for four seconds and breathe out for eight seconds.

Fear

Fear is another big emotion that can sometimes feel like an enemy. It can creep into your consciousness, stopping you from taking action, but this does not mean fear is entirely negative. It can be a protector too and has been keeping humans safe from things like wild animals, open water or flames for thousands of years. But if we don't rein in our fear, it can completely control our minds and limit the quality of our lives. We must be mindful of catastrophising, as we may miss out on opportunities, new experiences or adventures. If your fears turn into phobias (extreme or irrational fears), it might be worth seeking help. Find out more about phobias on p108.

An example of catastrophising

"I have a maths exam on Friday – I'll walk into the room and go blank. I won't even get marks for the working out because I'll forget everything. The invigilators will sense I don't know a thing and will stare at me disapprovingly. I am going to fail all my exams, not just maths. Well, that's college and university out the window . . ."

Whenever you find yourself catastrophising, remind yourself that these are just thoughts, and you don't have to listen to them. Our brains can sometimes make incorrect judgements and assumptions and no matter how strong these thoughts are, they can't predict the future.

Become the boss of fear

Fear can be such a strong and draining feeling. But, believe it or not, you can control it, especially when you get to grips with the idea of living outside your comfort zone. Have you ever heard of the 'learning zone model'?

The learning zone model is divided into three: the comfort zone, fear zone and growth zone.

If you are thinking about how to move through the different zones, it's all in your decisions. Did you know that making a decision is an act against fear itself? Many of us stay unsure and indecisive because it feels safer than committing to one outcome. We worry about making the wrong decision or failing. But deciding something (whatever the outcome) means we take back control.

The learning zone model

Growth zone

You try new things, take risks and make mistakes, but this is all part of the learning process. In this zone, you defy your fears and challenge yourself to set goals and do hard things. You grow in understanding yourself and the world around you and learn new skills along the way.

Fear zone

You are exposed to something you are unfamiliar with. Fear presents itself and alerts you to all the things you don't know, are unsure of or can't control. You begin to avoid the thing causing you to feel fearful.

Comfort zone

You are safe and feel in control. Although this zone can get a bad rep, it is not a bad place. It is a space where you can perform well and have confidence in what you know. But staying here too long can mean you're not learning new things or expanding your experiences; this can stunt your growth.

> **"FEEL the FEAR and DO IT anyway."**
> Susan Jeffers

Failing is human

When you make a decision or do something that challenges you, there will always be a risk of failure. But what's so bad about that? Why are we so scared of it? Why do we give it so much power over us? So many people struggle with the fear of failure, making mistakes and not being perfect enough. Striving for perfection is exhausting, so how about we don't do it? It is strange how we put expectations on ourselves but not on others. We would rather be around people who are fun or open or honest than perfect human beings! We see making mistakes as this horrible, scary beast, but so many of the things we enjoy were created by accident.

Play-Doh

Noah McVicker ran a soap-manufacturing company and had invented a new type of wallpaper-cleaning soap at his factory. Many homes in the 1930s used a coal-powered heating system, so wallpaper was often stained with soot. However, after World War II, homes started to be heated with natural gas and soot was no longer an issue, so the company struggled. Noah's sister-in-law, Kay Zufall, was a nursery teacher. She gave the non-toxic wallpaper cleaner to the kids, and they enjoyed moulding it into various shapes. Kay persuaded Noah to relaunch the cleaning product as a children's toy and suggested the name Play-Doh!

The chocolate chip cookie

Yup, the world's most beloved biscuit was invented by accident. In 1937, innkeeper Ruth Wakefield was making butter cookies for her guests when she decided they should be chocolate instead. She cut a bar of chocolate into tiny pieces and threw them into the cookie dough, thinking they would melt. To her surprise, the chocolate chips kept their form and her guests absolutely loved them. People came to the Toll House Inn specially to eat them!

5...4...3...2...1 GO! GO! GO!

The five second rule

You may feel afraid but that doesn't need to stop you. Remember, the act of failing does not make you a failure. Silence your inner critic. The amazing broadcaster Mel Robbins came up with a handy trick called the 'five second rule'. Mel realised that when something needs to be done, the longer you wait before taking action, the more you will feel anxiety, fear and dread. With her five second rule, Mel encourages people to outsmart fear by counting backwards from five and then cracking on with it. Maybe you want to contribute in class, have a difficult conversation with a friend or are putting off cleaning your room. Do not give yourself time to overthink and talk yourself out of it. Take a deep breath, count backwards from five and do it!

REFLECTION

Put mistakes in your toolbox. The fear of failing does not need to control you. Next time you make a mistake, why not probe it? Curiously ask, **"What can I learn from you?"** Your mistakes could be the clues that lead to a new discovery about yourself.

Reflect on a mistake (which felt like the worst thing ever at the time). Can you look at it in a new light? Did it teach you anything?

Activity time: *The big questions*

Some adults appear to know all the answers to life's most difficult questions. But don't forget that much of their wisdom has developed through learning from their mistakes. Having honest conversations with the grown-ups in your life can help you understand the humanity in making mistakes and how common they are. Use the following questions as a starting point but get creative with your own:

- How do you feel about mistakes and failure?
- Do you have any favourite mistakes or failures?
- Why are we taught to fear making mistakes?
- Why did they happen? What did you learn from them?

Fear-driven or growth-inspired?

The time has come to ask whether most of your decisions are driven by fear or inspired by growth. When we allow fear to drive our decision making, we limit ourselves to what feels safe and comfortable. With a growth-inspired decision you put your learning and progress above your fear. Fear will still crop up but that's totally okay. You don't need to ignore or dismiss fear; let yourself feel it and continue to fulfil your intentions.

JOURNAL TIME: Choose growth not fear

Have a look at the table below and see how fear-driven decisions can become growth-inspired ones. In your journal, complete the table with your examples of each type of decision.

FEAR-DRIVEN DECISIONS	GROWTH-INSPIRED DECISIONS
Avoiding speaking up in science and maths classes because everyone thinks they are harder, and you don't want to get the answer wrong.	
Saying no to trying out a new activity for fear that you won't be good at it.	

The Girl in the Arena

It is not the critic who counts;
not the girl who points out how the strong girl stumbles,
or where the doer of deeds could have done them better.

The credit belongs to the girl who is actually in the arena,
whose face is marred by dust and sweat and blood.

Who strives valiantly; who errs, who comes short again and again,
because there is no effort without error and shortcoming;
but who does actually strive to do the deeds.

Who knows great enthusiasms, the great devotions;
who spends herself in a worthy cause.

Who at the best knows in the end the triumph of high achievement,
and who at the worst, if she fails, at least fails while daring greatly,
so that her place will never be with those cold and timid souls
who neither know victory nor defeat.

*Adapted from Theodore Roosevelt's
'The Man in the Arena'*

Everyone has mental health

Yes, you read that right. Everyone has mental health because we all have minds. The issue is that sometimes 'mental health' and 'mental illness' are used interchangeably as if they are the same thing. Let's clarify the terms.

Mental health means our mental wellbeing; it encompasses our thoughts and emotions and our ability to overcome difficulties and understand the world around us. Our mental health exists on a spectrum ranging from good to poor. Good mental health helps you feel confident, act calmly and think positively about yourself and the world around you. If someone has poor mental health, their thoughts and feelings can become difficult to cope with.

Mental illness describes many different conditions, such as depression or anxiety, that affect how a person thinks, feels, behaves or interacts with others. People struggling with mental illness might not enjoy doing the things they previously loved or might struggle to control how they feel or behave.

⚠️ It is important to know that some mental health conditions require professional support.

Coping with your emotions

In this chapter, we've considered some anger-taming, mood-lifting and fear-challenging strategies that I hope you find useful. Here are some other activities and practices that can help you cope with overwhelming feelings. You do not have to do ALL of these things (exhausting, much?) but try some out and continue with what sticks and works for you.

> "We can't determine our emotions, but we can choose our attitudes and actions."
> *Gary Chapman*

Get physical
The challenge with recommending physical activity is that we're made to think we should only be active for how we look – to have toned arms, a snatched waist or whatever body type is trending right now. We often don't allow ourselves to enjoy being wildly energetic and experience just how helpful movement can be for our minds.

Honest buddy
Find someone that can be honest and rational with you whenever your anxiety is getting out of line. This has to be someone you feel comfortable 'going there with' (meaning you can bare your emotions to them). They give space for your feelings, but they are also able to challenge your emotions with rational thought.

Meditation
Quieten your brain by engaging with mindfulness. This means becoming more aware and present in the moment rather than having your thoughts drag you into the past or race forward into the future. There are many ways to explore mindfulness and meditation. It might be a challenge to get your mind to a place where it's quiet but why not give it a go? It could be useful.

Phobias

Phobias are an extreme form of fear. They are a type of anxiety disorder, which is a mental health condition. A phobia is more than a simple fear; it can force a person to organise their life around avoiding the thing that scares them. When it comes to phobias, the issue is not that you aren't brave enough — you might just need extra support to understand and overcome the extreme fear you feel. This is not something you have to work out alone. If you think you have a phobia and it's impacting your life, it may be helpful speaking to a GP.

Anxiety disorders

If you ever go from feeling anxious to having any of the following symptoms, it might be time to get some support from a GP. People feel anxiety in a variety of ways. It might feel completely emotional or you might experience physical symptoms with it. If you are struggling with your anxiety, then you should see your GP. Some of the following symptoms could be linked to something else entirely, so talking to a doctor will help you work out what's going on.

- Nausea, stomach pain, diarrhoea or vomiting
- Compulsive feelings*
- Feeling like you are outside your own body
- Heart racing and chest pains
- Avoiding certain situations, activities or people
- Trouble sleeping
- Headache
- Self-harming
- Difficulty concentrating
- Sweating
- Obsessive thoughts**
- Low appetite

*Feeling like you have to do particular things, otherwise there will be bad consequences.
**Thoughts that won't leave you alone.

 If you're at all worried or unsure about your feelings, it is really important to speak to your GP. They will provide you with the guidance and support you need.

Depression

Feeling sad or low from time to time is a normal part of the human experience. However, it's important to recognise that if you're feeling this way a lot or if it is affecting your daily life, then you should seek help.

Possible signs of depression

- Low self-esteem (thinking you are horrible and your life is pointless)
- Insomnia (getting little to no sleep)
- Gaining or dropping weight excessively
- Thinking about harming yourself
- No longer enjoying the activities you normally love
- Feeling hopeless about the future
- Self-harming
- Feeling unable to get out of bed

Eating disorders and body dysmorphia

You may have heard of eating disorders – the most well-known being anorexia nervosa and bulimia nervosa – but disordered eating exists on a spectrum and includes more subtle issues around food. Body dysmorphia is when a person spends a lot of time worrying about the appearance of their body, their weight or specific features they perceive as 'flaws'. Again, these issues can vary in severity drastically.

It is important to remember that even if you are a 'healthy' weight, you may still have an eating disorder if some of the points on the right are an issue for you. You don't have to be thin for your health to be at risk.

Possible signs of an eating disorder

- **Anxiety or obsession around food.**
- **Binge eating** – episodes of uncontrolled eating.
- **Restrictive eating** – this could be the amount or types of food.
- **Making yourself sick after eating.**
- **Negative body image** – not liking how you look or thinking you are 'too fat'.
- **Taking too many laxatives or other medications.**
- **Your period stopping or becoming irregular** when it was previously present or regular.
- **Excessive exercise** – there is no defined limit for this but if you feel stressed or anxious when you miss a workout, this could be a clue.
- **Symptoms related to extreme hunger or malnutrition** – dizziness, poor concentration, nausea or feeling tired.

Globally, around 1 in 12 people will develop an eating disorder at some point in their lives. If you worry a lot about the way you look, the amount or types of food you eat or the amount of exercise you do, it is a good idea to speak to a GP.

Self-harm

For some people, physical pain can be a distraction from emotional pain. Self-harm is often a symptom of other conditions, such as **depression** or **anxiety**. Sometimes people who feel they lack control self-harm because it is something they have complete control over. Others might feel that they are bad people and deserve to be hurt.

> Self-harm may feel like a coping mechanism, but it is always an issue that you should talk to a trusted adult or GP about.

What will happen at the GP appointment?

Your GP will have an initial chat with you on the phone or face to face. You can usually ask for one or the other. During the appointment, you can explore your feelings and symptoms and the GP might suggest one of a number of different strategies:

Counselling – This might be at your school or externally.

Psychotherapy – This is 'talking therapy', where you speak to a qualified and accredited practitioner and explore your feelings. There are many different types of psychotherapy, such as CBT (cognitive behavioural therapy), which can be helpful in dealing with negative thought patterns.

Additional therapies – Your GP may have access to forms of art, music and drama therapy, which give people a creative outlet and help them manage their mental health.

Medication – You have probably heard about medication being used to treat mental health illnesses. While prescription drugs are occasionally used to treat young people in specific situations, your GP is likely to try talking therapies first.

Confidentiality

After the initial conversation with your GP, they will follow up with you regularly to see how you're doing. There are rules and laws about confidentiality that are there to protect you, but it is also important for you to be able to seek help and have your privacy respected. If you feel very strongly about not including your parents or guardians in discussions about your mental or physical health, there are instances in which you could speak to your GP confidentially, but this will depend on the circumstances. Your GP will always explain if and why they need to include a parent or guardian and wherever possible would try to respect your wishes.

Sleep

The power in your snooze

Getting good sleep is a critical part of your overall health, but especially your mental health, as it plays a major role in regulating your mood and emotions. So much of our everyday lives can be unpredictable and uncertain, so for some people being able to control little details, like when they go to bed and wake up or what their bedtime routine is, can help regulate feelings of worry and fear.

Creating your night routine

There are hundreds upon thousands of online videos of different morning routines from the 4am 'billionaire morning routine' to the 5am 'IT girl morning routine'. But you don't need to get up at the crack of dawn to be successful; the real secret to a great morning is a good bedtime routine!

Things to avoid before bed

- Caffeine after lunch
- Heavy meals
- Stressful conversations
- Vigorous exercise before bed
- Using bed for activities other than sleep, such as homework or gaming

Things to help you sleep

- If you can, spend some time outdoors after school
- Gentle movement
- A well-ventilated room that is not too hot or cold
- Ambient or white noise
- Make sure your room is dark when you go to sleep
- Progressive muscle relaxation (PMR) – once in bed, try tensing the different muscles in your body for about five seconds and then relax them. PMR has been shaown to decrease stress and anxiety levels and promote relaxation.

Sleep early

Let's be honest, you can only really get up early without feeling like a sleep-deprived zombie if you go to bed early. I know it's hard to accept . . . everyone's online in the evening, you've spent the whole day busy learning and now you finally have the evening to yourself. But going to bed early is one of the best ways to ensure you get enough sleep and wake up feeling well-rested and emotionally prepared to take on the challenges of the day.

Unplug

Electronic devices can cause insomnia because of the blue light they emit. It suppresses your body's production of melatonin (remember this sleep-regulating hormone?) and messes with your internal rhythm, making it harder to fall and stay asleep.

Declutter your mind

Let's say you're in bed at 9.30pm and sleep seems to be far away. Have you ever really wanted to get to sleep but felt like your mind would not shut off? You are not alone. Research shows that a lot of people can struggle to get a good night's rest because they find it difficult to quieten the mind. If this is you, you could try losing yourself in a good book, journalling or making a to-do list for the next day. Journalling can help you process things and make sense of the stray thoughts tumbling around your head. This might help to free up your mind and usher you into a zen mode, ready for bed.

"Once I get through my homework around six, I make some hot chocolate and watch some cosy vlogs on YouTube for a little while. It really helps me relax."
Niamh (15)

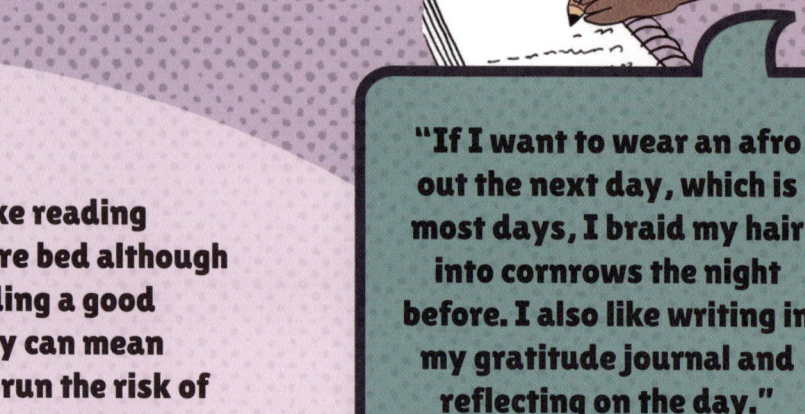

"If I want to wear an afro out the next day, which is most days, I braid my hair into cornrows the night before. I also like writing in my gratitude journal and reflecting on the day."
Titilayo (14)

"I like reading before bed although reading a good story can mean I run the risk of staying up to finish it."
Eden (13)

Activity time: Create your bedtime routine

What could you do to unwind and prepare for bed in the evening? Have you considered keeping a sleep diary? This can help you get to know the bedtime routine elements that work for you and what to avoid at night in your quest for a good night's sleep!

Remember, there is no such thing as a perfect bedtime routine. It is just about finding out what works for you.

Our feelings make us human

Your mind, mood and feelings are powerful. Having feelings makes us human, and experiencing intense emotions is nothing to be ashamed of. The emotions we have covered in this chapter – anger, fear and stress – are strong signals that communicate what we are experiencing. They can be very helpful. Anger can drive you to advocate for yourself and other people. Fear can alert you to real dangers that exist, such as fast cars on a busy road, and help you to be more attentive or cautious. You may not be able to control what you feel, but your emotions do not have to run your life. After acknowledging them, you have the power to decide what you do going forwards and how your feelings can be a force for good. Remember that you do not have to navigate overwhelming emotions by yourself. If you are struggling with stress, anxiety or any intense feelings, you are not alone and there is support out there. Everyone has mental health, and it is always wise to ask for help to take better care of yours.

"Education breeds **confidence**.
Confidence breeds *hope*.
Hope breeds *peace*."

Confucius

Chapter 6
School

Let's explore . . .
Dealing with pressure, failing and growing, skills and success and your career options.

You can find out more about getting involved in political change and activism in Chapter 7.

Across the globe, girls are in classrooms, raising their hands and contributing their views but there are still countries where they are denied the right to learn.

According to the United Nations, nearly 130 million girls are not enrolled in formal education. Your voice is powerful, and you can lend your skills, resources and time to support the global conversations and campaigns for girls' right to education.

Even in places where girls' schooling is a given, female education does not come without challenges and costs. There is huge hype around grades and performance – in primary school it's about getting the best SATs, then in secondary you're facing the monstrous GCSEs and after that it can feel like your whole future depends on whether your A-level results meet the entry requirements for your dream university or whatever you want to do next.

> "We cannot all succeed when half of us are held back."
> *Malala Yousafzai*

Dealing with pressure

It is a lot of pressure for anyone, but studies have shown that the mental health of girls is particularly affected by the pressures of academic achievement. This is linked to the constant demand on girls to be perfect, not only academically but in other aspects of life too. A combination of being afraid of the future, mounting pressures from parents and trying to survive a competitive school culture all add to the immense burden girls feel while navigating education.

Racism at school

Aside from the academic expectations and pressures, girls of ethnic backgrounds, particularly Black girls, often endure racist and unfair treatment within the school system, which severely damages their self-confidence and mental health.

The Child Q case

In 2022, the tragic case of 'Child Q' brought to national attention just how horribly young Black girls can be treated in schools. Child Q (so-called to protect her identity) was 15 years old when she was strip searched at school by two police officers without any other adults present. She had been sitting an exam when she was escorted out of the hall by police. Apparently, a member of staff thought she had drugs on her and called the police because they were concerned. The officer ordered a strip search and no drugs were found; Child Q was on her period at the time.

In March 2022, thousands of people took to the streets of London to protest against this unlawful behaviour and to show support for Child Q and her family. It is very important that girls can learn in environments where they feel safe, respected and protected. In Child Q's case, the teachers and staff supposed to look after her failed in their duty. But there are also many educators and school staff determined to help and support you through school. It is important to seek out help when you need it by talking to a trusted teacher, but also know you can question the actions and sayings of any adult that make you feel unsafe.

Living in poverty

Child poverty is on the rise and it can affect how a young person experiences education. Save the Children found that kids who come from lower income families are half as likely as their classmates to do well in school. This is because young people living in poverty may struggle with concentration, hunger, tiredness, ill health and bullying. School can be a lot to take on but there is support available. Some after-school clubs help young people with their learning, homework and extra-curricular interests.

If you are worried about food, clothing or issues around money, know that you can speak to a trusted teacher about your concerns. Some schools also offer breakfast clubs so you can start the day with a good meal, ready to learn. There is nothing to be embarrassed or ashamed about. School is there to support you both academically and personally.

Story time

I have two brothers; one is into aeronautical engineering (heavy on the maths and equations), and the other is into cybersecurity (and all things tech). I am constantly in awe of how their brains can manage and make sense of such complex numbers, statistics and codes. I praise them for it all the time because one of my strengths is writing, and I much prefer words to numbers. But there was a time when I didn't consider my strengths as important. At school, I used to think, "Okay sure, I like words and I know how to use them, but so does everyone else. Maths on the other hand? My brain could never; that is so much more difficult and impressive."

At school, I often felt ashamed of enjoying and excelling at arts subjects, like creative writing, English, and performing arts. I felt like I was taking the easy way out because I enjoyed 'soft' subjects that were not numerical or scientific.

REFLECTION

Think about the things you enjoy and do well, whether they are academic subjects, sports or extra-curricular activities.

Do you sometimes take your stengths for granted?

When I started having conversations with my brothers about education, I was surprised that they were amazed by how much information I could read, take in and recall from memory or how quickly and well I could write. They found the thought of writing an essay, let alone a book, absolutely impossible. My brothers made me realise that writing isn't easy or basic. It is a strength. And yes, it might flow quite easily for me, but that's something to celebrate!

123

BUILD ON YOUR STRENGTHS

Learning, failing and growing

Sometimes we limit ourselves to learning or doing things that we are naturally good at. Why? Well, because it's an 'easy' win. With little or no effort, you might be able to paint a picture, win the debate or crack the code. While this is amazing, you don't have to stop there. Not every talent is immediately obvious or easy to learn, but growth comes when we are willing to try something new or hard and become better with practice.

School is for learning, failing and ultimately growing. Though it can sometimes feel like everyone is expected to know all the right answers, this is not true. If everyone already knew everything, what would be the point of school, college or university?

Who comes into this world already knowing Pythagoras' theorem or how to analyse structure in poetry? We all have knowledge gaps, and school is a place to build our understanding. Remember what we discussed in Chapter 5 about the fear of failure? Failing is bound to happen when you attempt to go from your comfort zone into your learning zone. Everyone will make mistakes and there is no shame in that.

Studying and homework

I remember a meme going around once that defined studying as a combination of "student + dying". But honestly, studying does not have to be a torturous experience. Understanding the difference between studying and revising might be the key to hacking student life.

- Studying is learning something new or increasing your knowledge of a familiar topic.
- Revision is relearning or going over things you already know through studying.

Homework plan

This is simply a schedule that outlines when you will study. A homework plan does not have to be super detailed or colour co-ordinated per subject if that's not your thing. It can be as basic or as complicated as you like, but you could start with the following:

- Write down key dates of any class tests or mock exams.
- Block out time for school and extra-curricular activities as well as fun and rest.
- Do you work better in the morning or evening? Can you study right after school, or do you need a break first?
- Understand your learning habits to get the most out of your schedule.
- How much time do you need for each task? You could ask a teacher what they recommend.
- Try the 'pomodoro technique'! This time management method breaks work into intervals of 25 minutes separated by short breaks (about ten minutes). It helps you focus without getting distracted.
- Find someone (like a parent or sibling) to hold you to your homework plan. They can help you stay on track and it might keep them off your back during rest time.

Activity time
Build a homework plan

Here is an example student timetable. Use it as a starting point for your study plan. Remember, you can always rework the plan as you go if something is not working well.

HOMEWORK

NAME _____

	MONDAY	TUESDAY	WEDNESDAY	THURSDAY	FRIDAY
ACTIVITIES					
HOMEWORK					
FUN/REST					

Ideas for your 10-minute study break

- Have a snack
- Dance to loud music
- Have a drink
- Do a crossword puzzle
- Lie on the grass and look at the sky
- Read a magazine
- Stroke a pet
- Hug something cuddly
- Message a friend
- Go for a short walk

Create your study space

Now, you've got your homework schedule in hand but is the vibe right? Have a look around your environment and ask yourself if the atmosphere is going to help you think, study and learn.

Location – the kitchen table, your room, the library – there are many places to set up a homework station. Find a quiet and comfortable place where you can focus. Clear the clutter but stock up with important stationery supplies.

Brain food – make sure you've got a stock of fruit, nuts and dark chocolate in your study space; these foods will help power your mind.

Music – some people love listening to music while they study; others simply can't concentrate. I say, stick with what works, but having the TV on in the background probably won't help . . .

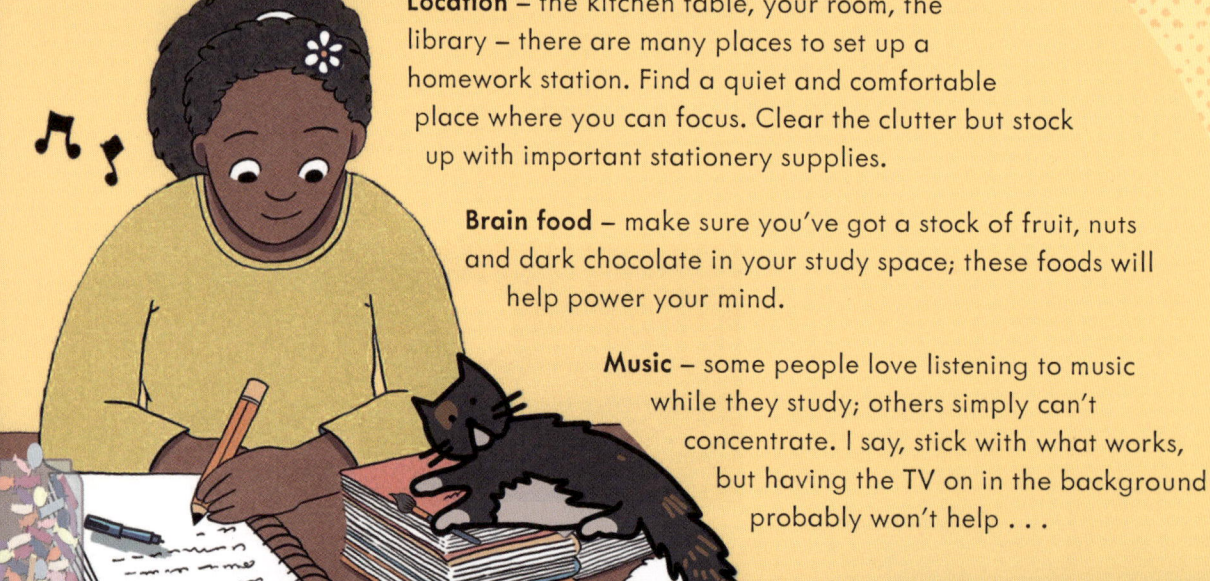

Discipline

You have created a homework schedule, and your study space is set up – post-its, fruit, nuts and all. But here comes the difficult part – doing the work. This is where discipline comes in and we need it to get through challenging or boring tasks. At times there will be many other things you'd rather be doing or places you'd rather be but try to stick to the schedule. Your hard work will pay off.

Activity time
Stay disciplined

Research shows that rewards are a great way to motivate learners.

What are some of the ways you can reward yourself for sticking to your study schedule?

> "Many highly talented, brilliant, creative people think they're not because the thing they were good at, at school, wasn't valued"
> — Ken Robinson

What if I don't succeed at school?

While some people are pressed and stressed about performing well in school, there are others who, well, couldn't really care less. This happens for many reasons.

> "I can spend hours sat in front of my books and nothing goes in."
> Rochelle (15)

> "Everyone else gets it and I just don't."
> Adelaide (11)

> "I am always trying to outperform and please my parents, but it never feels enough."
> Grace (15)

It is important to talk to teachers about any problems you might be encountering at school. There is no value in suffering in silence. If it feels like everyone else has hacked the subject or the studying, it might be helpful to team up with a classmate or ask your friends who are doing well to support you. It is okay to ask for help.

Success on your own terms

It is also really important to define what success means to you. A lot of emphasis is put on getting the best grades but school offers more than that. You learn to communicate with others, navigate playground conflict, work independently and in a team. The truth is, not everyone flourishes in school environments because they have skills that are better explored and celebrated elsewhere. Some young people, particularly those who are neurodivergent, may find that being in a school environment overwhelms their senses or negatively impacts their mental health. If this is you, support is out there. Speak to a parent or trusted adult about how you are feeling and check out the resource section at the back of the book for helpful websites.

There are loads of non-academic skills that are not typically celebrated in school, such as electronics, cosmetology, culinary arts, carpentry and vlogging, to name a few. It is no surprise that many people find their place in the world after leaving school. If you feel like this might be you, don't worry too much. Focus on the things you do well, try your best and forget the rest.

"Success is a deeply personal matter. For some people it's fame or wealth or possessions or popularity or qualifications. But for me, success is something far simpler; it's about knowing you've done your best irrespective of what other people think of you."
Tim Bowler

Dear High-achiever,

Even if you do not achieve,
A single thing more
In this lifetime,
You have done enough.
Being here is enough.
Keeping on is enough.

Teach your tongue to sing your own praise.
Turn from the world's greedy, all-consuming gaze.
For they will never be satisfied,
They will always demand more,
An encore of your suffering,
Camouflaged as achieving.

Anonymous

JOURNAL TIME
Your definition of success

What is your definition of success? List the things that make you feel strong and successful.

Learning outside the classroom

Learning does not have to stop when school is out! In fact, for anyone reading whose learning style clashes with the way school works, it can be liberating to know there are other methods to build your knowledge and develop yourself.

Visit local sites
These could be theatres, museums, heritage sites, religious buildings or botanical gardens.

Challenge yourself
Build your confidence by engaging with outdoor activities and try something new, like den building, rock-climbing or painting.

Develop your skills
You could try organising an expedition, plan for an author to visit your local youth club or library, practise painting or make music.

Build your knowledge
Watch documentaries or listen to podcasts. You could take an online course or try a workshop on anything from creative writing to pottery.

Life after school

If the thought of waving goodbye to pestering teachers, bland school meals and petty playground squabbles sounds like a dream, then you are probably really looking forward to life after school. I totally understand this because school can be really tough, but for all its trouble, it brings a sense of certainty and continuity. Up until you finish secondary school, you know you'll spend most of your days in the classroom and what topics you'll be learning about. The choices you make after secondary school mark the beginning of a lifetime of making adult decisions. This may be a long way off for you, but it can be helpful to have an idea about what is to come in the years ahead.

JOURNAL TIME
Action plan

Today, commit to learning and developing yourself beyond the classroom. List one new skill you are interested in building and write out your action plan for it.

What are my options after Year 11?

Get a job and take a work-related course like an OCR National, BTEC or City and Guilds qualification. These are practical, fun courses that help you develop real-world skills in various areas from enterprise and marketing to sports science and health and social care.

If you want to go to university but continue working, degree apprenticeships are available in many different sectors, such as finance, engineering, nursing, teaching, nuclear science and law.

Stay in school by going to a college or sixth form and study full-time courses. These are level 3 qualifications (A-levels and BTEC) in a wide range of subjects from English literature to chemistry, performing arts and economics. Most (but not all) young people who take A-levels and BTEC courses are considering going to university.

Begin an apprenticeship or traineeship if you want a more 'hands-on' approach to your career. You will gain a qualification in an area you are interested in while getting paid and receiving practical on-job experience.

Now, deciding which path to take is entirely your choice. But in order to make an informed decision, it helps to expose yourself to all the possible options, research them thoroughly and speak to people who have taken a path that you're curious about. You may not know anyone with a job you're interested in, but the internet has given us a great advantage. You can read articles, watch videos or listen to podcasts to find out more about different careers.

Your career journey

There are many things in life that bring happiness – think rainbows, puppies, apple crumble with custard(!) – including a fulfilling career. It's true that our worth and value should not be tied to the work we do or how well we do it. But you will spend a lot of time at work, so it should ideally be something that you enjoy.

Do you have an idea of what career you would like to pursue? Maybe you don't know just yet, but you have a sense of what interests you and what you are good at. You might be a bit of a counsellor and great at giving advice. Maybe you love creating things from scratch or cooking for people. Perhaps you're the most organised among your friends. Pay attention to the things you enjoy. Don't take them for granted or write them off as unimportant because they seem to 'come easy' to you.

There is always that one person who knows exactly what they want to do with the rest of their lives, but most of us do not have a clue and may stumble into a career we really enjoy. It could even be that what you want to do does not exist yet! Our world is constantly evolving and many roles and jobs that are popular now were relatively unknown just a few years ago. Here are some examples:

Can you think of any more?

- Podcast producer
- Vlogger/blogger
- Artificial intelligence engineer
- Coder
- Drone pilot

JOURNAL TIME
Discover your skills

Let's ease up on the stress and anxiety that can come with facing the 'what do you want to do with your life' question. Instead, take a deep breath and focus on answering these four questions:

1. What do you enjoy doing?
2. Which skills are your strongest?
3. What skills are in demand right now?
4. How can you build those skills?

21st century skills

I often suggest that young people should try not to think strictly in terms of a dream career. It might be more helpful to think about your interests and how you can build some of the 21st century skills that are in high demand.

When we think in terms of building a diverse set of skills instead of one specific career, we give ourselves the space to pivot if the career we initially thought of as 'the one' ends up being the wrong fit.

The 4Cs

The 4Cs encompass the most essential of the 21st century skills. These key skills will help young people to succeed and find their place in the world.

Critical thinking
Being able to read, analyse and evaluate information.

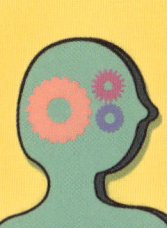

Collaboration
Working in a team with individuals of diverse abilities and backgrounds.

Communication
Presenting your ideas articulately in verbal or written form.

Creativity
Coming up with innovative ideas and solutions.

Activity time
Exploring the 4Cs

Which of the 4Cs do you need to develop? What kinds of activities and hobbies will give you the opportunity to build on them?

Example: To develop my critical thinking abilities, I will read more widely and expose myself to views and opinions that are different to my own.

JOURNAL TIME
Create a career mind map

Copy out the below mind map in your journal. Draw lines coming off each bubble and fill in your answers.

- What are you great at?
- What do you enjoy doing?
- What kind of impact do you want to have in the world?
- CAREER MIND MAP
- What do people say you're good at?
- What do you care about?

If you are really stuck, you could find an online career personality test. But remember that your prospects aren't determined by artificial intelligence.

The makings of a great plan

At this point we've made mind maps of your hobbies, areas of interest and possible careers. Now you're armed with enough information to start crafting your goals!

1. Celebrate where you are now!
Take a moment to reflect on the present and then think back to where you used to be and appreciate that your journey is already in full swing.

2. List out your career aspirations
Think over the activities you've done so far in this chapter; do any industries stand out? How do you want to feel at work? What impact do you want to have?

3. Play the long game
What long-term goals do you need to achieve your dream career? Maybe it's going to college or university or finding an apprenticeship.

4. Also play the short game!
Think about the things that will help with your long-term goals. It could be career research or speaking to someone with a job you're interested in. If you want to develop a particular skill, your short-term goal could be practising it or watching tutorials on how to improve.

It's your future

Hopefully, reading and working through this chapter has given you a better idea of your strengths, passions and interests but also served as a reminder that life is so much more than academic achievement. Schoolin' school life is about enjoying the learning journey and not making it all about the destination. The aim of this chapter is to get you to imagine what school would be like if failing was not a concern – how much more brave, adventurous or at peace would you be?

Now you know how to make a homework plan and create a great study space for yourself outside of school. If academia is not your strongest point, that is okay. When you define success for yourself and embrace your strengths and weaknesses, you can find your place in the world by working out where your abilities will be celebrated.

If thinking about the future feels daunting, remember that it is okay to be unclear about which industry, job or courses you want to be involved with. I'll let you in on a secret – most of us are figuring it out as we go along. You can pivot (change course) at any time, and you do not have to stick with one job or career path for the rest of your life. Only a small percentage of graduates have a job related to their degree, and many successful people do not even have degrees. Lots of in-demand jobs don't require degrees but use practical skills, for example plumbing, carpentry or cosmetics. A huge part of stepping into your power as you evolve is recognising that your path will not be like everyone else's.

Embrace your authentic journey.

"Before you call yourself a Christian, Buddhist, Muslim, Hindu or any other theology, **learn to be human** first."

Shannon L. Alder

Chapter 7
Beliefs

Let's explore . . . your values, tricky moral dilemmas, religion, politics and becoming a change agent.

Ever wondered what shapes your beliefs or asked yourself why you think in a particular way? Our thoughts and ideas don't slip into our heads accidentally. People, institutions, books and experiences can make our belief systems change over time. This part of the book looks at one of the most beautiful yet complex parts of being human – our minds, thoughts, values, morals and beliefs.

As humans, we have the power of imagination and complex thought, allowing us to form strong opinions, which can unite or divide us.

Values

Values are a set of beliefs based on the things that matter most to a person. There are no rules – values can be anything from spending quality time with family and friends to having a strong work ethic or having a good time and living your best life! The important thing about values is that we all have them. Have you identified what yours are?

Exploring your values

You might not realise it, but you are a member of certain groups, communities and societies. Your family, your school, your neighbourhood, the country you are from or grew up in, your faith community (if you have one) – all of these places, people and systems have an influence on you and your values. As part of growing up, you may look back at the values and beliefs you have had since childhood and decide to embrace, challenge, reject or tweak them a little bit.

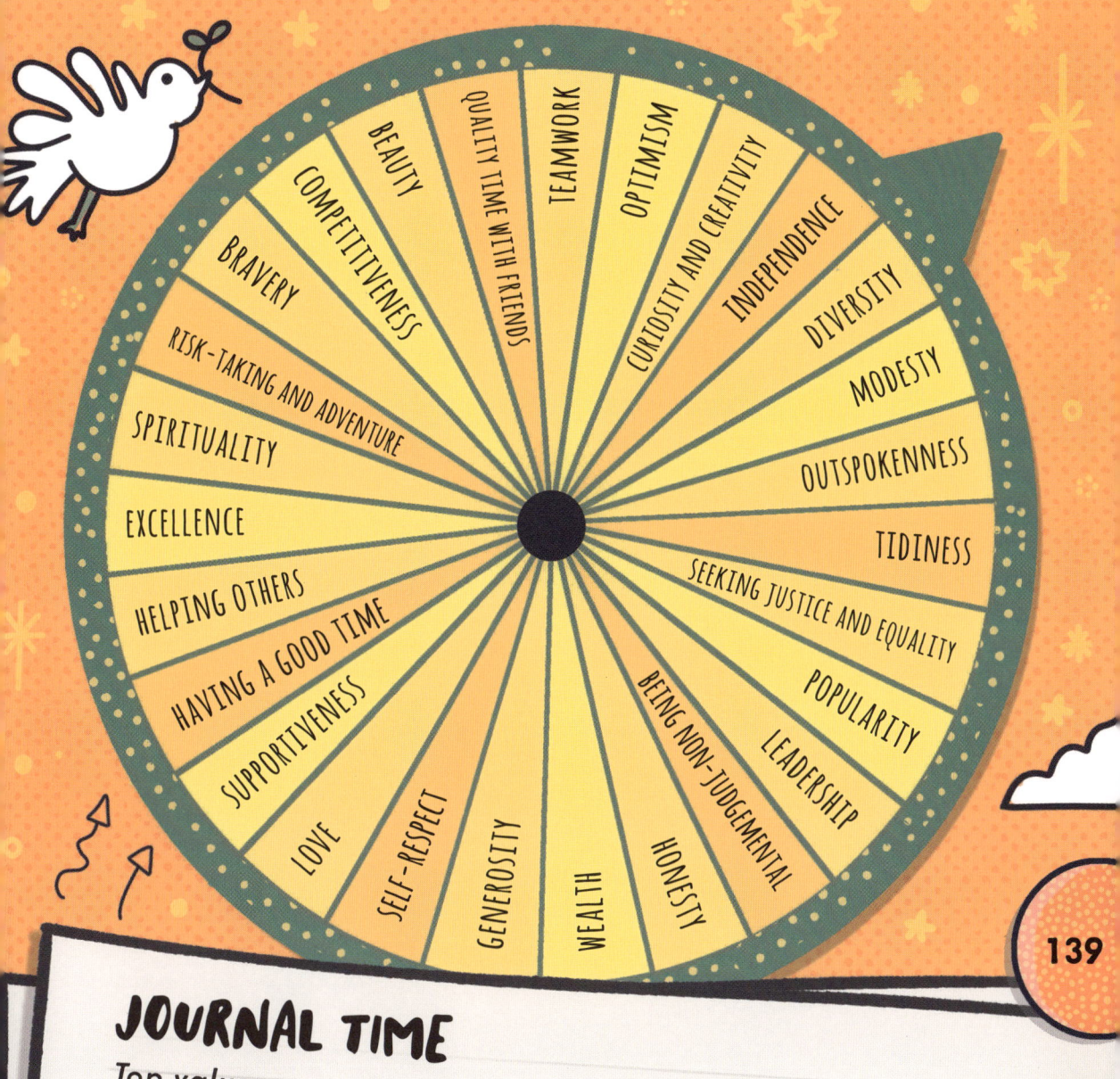

JOURNAL TIME
Top values

Take a look at the values in the wheel and list your top ten. Feel free to add your own! Now, highlight your top five. Think about how these top five values could play out in your everyday life. It might help to think about your daily priorities!

Here's one of mine — I value honesty with myself and other people. This means I am willing to admit my flaws and mistakes, but it also means I aim to answer honestly when I am asked difficult questions by others. I won't lie to them, even if it risks hurting their feelings, but I will speak the truth with love.

Being a 'high-value' girl

There are loads of conversations happening across social media about what it means to be a 'high-value woman' – the term has about 106 million views on TikTok alone. The issue is that this idea of being 'high-value' is often based on a girl attracting and keeping the attention of others. The online focus on appearance, complying with a stereotypical view of femininity that tells girls to be quiet and unopinionated (and therefore unproblematic), is a far cry and distraction from the radiant list of values we considered earlier in the chapter.

Being a real high-value girl is about choosing yourself. It means you rank high on your own 'value scoreboard', one entirely of your choosing. But please don't get me wrong – if wearing cute outfits is YOUR thing or if looking after your appearance makes YOU feel empowered or strong or beautiful, more power to you! Deciding to be intentionally feminine (however you define it) can be YOUR decision and have nothing to do with pleasing other people.

> "Who taught you that the value of a [girl] is the ratio of her waist to her hips... and the volume of her lips? Your math is dangerously wrong, her value is nothing less than infinite."
>
> Della Hicks-Wilson

Growing up as a young Black girl, I often felt like I was not allowed to look feminine because it was not my aesthetic to own. It seemed like I had to wear tracksuits and trainers (which I also love by the way) if I didn't want anyone to raise an eyebrow. When I started putting effort into my appearance, I was made to feel like I was trying to be what I was not. A part of reclaiming my value now is wearing colours and embracing clothes I used to be shamed out of wearing because of my curvy physique and my race.

What if my values are changing?

You are growing, finding your voice and becoming your own person, but it can be tempting to pretend your values aren't really changing or being challenged. Sometimes it feels easier to accept the values of your friends, family or the popular view. Avoiding conflict or difficult conversations about your new beliefs and convictions might feel good in the moment but keeping up a pretence can be exhausting and unsettling.

> "When we were growing up, my parents would make racist jokes about our Indian next-door neighbours. My dad made mean comments about the way their food smelled and said they were stinking up our neighbourhood and didn't belong here."
>
> Angie, 14

In Angie's case, her value of accepting diversity among people was being challenged by her parents' behaviour. You might feel that speaking up would be rebellious or disrespectful, but that's not true. Think about using your voice to let the people around you know that your values have changed and explain why their behaviour is hurtful to you.

Activity time
Conflict of values

Let's imagine that a conflict has arisen between you and someone you care about due to your changing beliefs. How could you address this situation without escalating it? Examples might include saying:

"Hey, I actually don't agree with that."
"Actually, I don't think that's true any more. Here's what I think . . ."
Add some of your own . . .

Maybe you don't feel ready to have a conversation about your change in values because it could result in an argument that you just do not have the energy for. That is totally okay; be sure to pick your battles and choose when you want to speak up. Always remember that you are in control here.

Morals

While values are what you personally consider to be important, morals tend to be shared by larger groups of people. Morals dictate standards of behaviour that are necessary for societies to live together in harmony. Morals are formed out of personal values, so they can differ between people. But in most societies, there is an agreed set of morals that influence laws.

Here are some common social morals that have become laws in the UK:

Do not destroy property

The Criminal Damage Act 1971 makes it a criminal offence to damage or destroy property belonging to someone else without a lawful excuse.

Being dishonest is wrong

The Fraud Act 2006 and **the Theft Act 1968** define fraud as being dishonest and using deception for your own advantage or to cause another person loss.

Respect difference

Hate crime happens when people's differences are not respected. Instead, they experience acts of violence and hostility because of characteristics like their race, religion, sexual orientation or disability. **The Crime and Disorder Act 1998** specifically highlights offences targeting people of diverse racial and religious backgrounds.

Can you think of some others? If not, do some research and write down what you find.

Changing moral codes

It is also important to say that society and the law do not always get the moral code right. Some behaviours, values and attitudes that used to be acceptable are now regarded as horrendous and immoral. There was a devastating 400-year period in human history, from the 15th to the 19th century, when people and politicians in European and American society thought it was morally and legally acceptable for more than 15 million women, men and children to be made slaves. Black Africans were stripped of their dignity, human rights and identity. They were treated like animals – chained and shipped off to wealthy western countries and their colonies, including America, Britain, Belgium, France and the Netherlands, or sent to work on plantations owned by rich Europeans or Americans.

Did you know that there was a time when it was lawful and morally acceptable for women to be beaten by their husbands? Societal attitudes, and eventually laws, gradually changed concerning this issue, but it could not have happened without the collective of angry women, including survivors and allies, who bravely rallied together to make change happen.

"Human MORALITY is unthinkable without EMPATHY."

Frans de Waal

A brief timeline of domestic violence laws in the UK

1782
A judge came up with the 'rule of thumb', which stated that a man could beat his wife; he just had to make sure the rod was not thicker than his thumb. This common law principle was held throughout the 19th century.

1895
A curfew on wife-beating was introduced. This law made it illegal for a man to hit his wife between 10pm and 7am. The law was only introduced because the noises made by women in pain were keeping neighbours awake.

1971–1975

144

Various incredible organisations began advancing women's rights. Refuge, Rape Crisis, Women's Aid and Rights of Women were established. They pressured Parliament to discuss the issue of domestic violence.

1976
The first EVER UK law dedicated to preventing domestic violence was created. It gave victims new rights and protections against abuse.

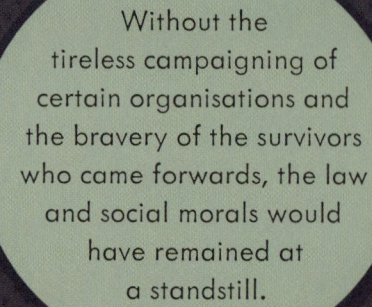

Without the tireless campaigning of certain organisations and the bravery of the survivors who came forwards, the law and social morals would have remained at a standstill.

It is important to note that a young person is considered a victim of domestic abuse if they harm themselves or witness harmful exchanges between their parents at home. While unfortunately domestic violence still happens, there are now ways for people to get help escaping from these situations and stopping abusers.

There are resources at the back of the book for anyone that may need help with these issues.

You can find a detailed timeline on the Centre for Women's Justice website, linked in the resource section.

Moral dilemmas

What happens when you find yourself having to navigate two conflicting morals – which one wins? How do you make that decision? This conflict is called a 'moral dilemma' and it can put you in a sticky situation. Moral dilemmas come in all shapes and sizes. Let's look at an example.

The Manchester conjoined twins

A pregnant woman named Rina discovered that she was having twin girls and that they were conjoined. In this case, it meant they shared a spine and a pelvis. The twins were named Mary and Jodie. Mary's heart, lungs and brain had not fully formed and she relied on the organs in Jodie's body to stay alive. The doctors believed that both babies would die unless an operation to separate them was performed. The operation would save Jodie's life. However, the twins' parents were Catholics and had different beliefs to the doctors; they did not agree to ending Mary's life, even if it would save Jodie's.

This was a difficult moral and ethical dilemma. The case went to court, where a judge ordered that the separation should go ahead, but the parents appealed the decision and a retrial happened in the Court of Appeal. It was an agonising case, but the senior judges rejected the appeal. Jodie and Mary went through a 20-hour operation – neurosurgeons separated all the bones, internal organs and blood vessels the twins shared. As a result, Mary died. Today Jodie is alive and living with her parents.

REFLECTION

Sometimes in life there are no right answers, just difficult choices.
What was the moral dilemma here?
Whose beliefs do you share? Why?
Is there anyone you strongly disagree with? Why is that?

Your moral compass

You might not know how you are going to respond to a situation until you are in it and are forced to make a split-second decision. It is worth thinking, reading and exploring different moral dilemmas to help develop your personal set of values and beliefs regarding what is right or wrong. This is your moral compass. It is driven by your intuition but also your religion, culture, family and upbringing.

Activity time
What would you do?

We've talked about your moral compass and navigating the tricky terrain of speaking up. Have a look at the following moral dilemmas and think about what you would do. I encourage you to discuss your answers with your friends or family. You might be surprised by them!

Reporting a crime

Your friend tells you they have committed a crime. They feel really guilty and are struggling to sleep at night. You are the only one who knows. The police come to your school asking anyone with information to come forward.

Do you:

Tell the police what you know?

Encourage your friend to confess but say that you will tell if they do not?

Keep quiet out of loyalty to your friend?

The friend in need

One of your friends is struggling with their mental health, and you're the only person they open up to. Some of the things they say really scare you, and you think they need help, but they tell you not to tell anyone.

Do you:

Call Childline for advice

Stay quiet

Speak to a trusted teacher or family member

The cheating student

Your friend is desperate to get a good grade on the upcoming maths test. During break, you both go to the classroom, and they ask you to watch the door while they quickly take pictures of the answers.

Do you refuse or go along with it so as not to upset your friend?

The sarcastic bestie

Your best friend is absolutely hilarious and always cracking jokes. But sometimes the jokes can go a little too far and involve making fun of other people. It makes you uncomfortable.

Do you say something or just laugh along?

Loose change

You buy something at your local supermarket store and the cashier gives you too much change.

Do you let them know or keep quiet and leave the store?

Religion

A person's values and morals can exist alongside their religion or faith. This world is made up of many pluralistic societies. A pluralistic society allows people of different values, cultures, ideas, classes and religions to live and work together. As a citizen of the world, it is important to be accepting and tolerant of the views of other people, whether or not you share them.

You may not be religious – perhaps you identify as agnostic (you neither believe or disbelieve in God) or atheist (you do not believe in God) – but it's likely that some of your neighbours, friends and family members will have a religion. It is not just about what you believe; religion can play a huge role in people's lifestyles too. It can dictate what people eat, how they dress, whether they show their hair and, of course, their moral code. Therefore, regardless of our own faith (or lack of faith), it is essential that we learn about different religions. Understanding the role they play in society will help us to be respectful and tolerant of other people's behaviour and choices.

> "My religion is very simple. My religion is kindness."
> *Dalai Lama*

The five big world religions

More than 85% of people in the world identify with a religion. There are over 4,000 recognised religions globally, but most of the world's population practise one of the following five major religions:

Christianity has the world's biggest faith group with about 2.38 billion people identifying as Christians. This religion is based on the teachings of Jesus of Nazareth. Christians believe that Jesus was chosen by God to save humans from sin.

Islam is the second biggest religion, practised by 1.91 billion people. The five pillars of Islam are: faith, prayer, almsgiving (charity), fasting and pilgrimage. The religion has origins in the Middle East and was revealed by the Prophet Muhammad.

Buddhism has a following of 507 million people. Buddhism originated in India and is based on the teachings of the Buddha. His teachings are principally about suffering – where it comes from and how to cure it.

Hinduism is practised by 1.16 billion people. It is the third largest religion and it began in India. Hindus believe in reincarnation (the soul is reborn) and karma (your actions decide your fate).

Judaism is practised by 14.6 million people. Jews believe in one God who has established a covenant (special agreement) with them; good deeds are rewarded and evil is punished.

How people practise their religion

Worship
Followers of a particular religion often come together to attend special services in a holy building. Here, people can attend classes to learn more about the religion, read sacred texts or practise religious rituals.

Religious holidays
Going on a religious holiday (sometimes called a retreat) is a special, fun and often relaxing way of connecting more deeply with your faith. Some people travel to places like Jerusalem, Mecca, Amritsar or Taizé to reflect on and develop their spirituality.

Festivals
Religious festivals can be a colourful, vibrant and exciting way to celebrate beliefs. These festivals often have special food, clothes, games and performances to honour their god(s). Did you know World Religion Day is the third Sunday in January? It's a day when people from all cultures and backgrounds celebrate the major faiths of the world.

Activity time
Religion discovery

Research the different places of worship and the types of services religious people attend.

Can you find at least three?

Can you find a religious festival that young people really enjoy attending?

What is special about it and why do young people love it?

Look up a religious holiday destination. What can you find out about the different activities people enjoy there?

Why religion?

While there are many young people who do not practise any religion, others may choose to commit to a religion for many different reasons. Some may have been raised in a religious family and so decide to hold on to these values. Others may have encountered difficulties in their personal life and have turned to religion for direction, or to make sense of their experiences. Some may have been introduced to religion through friends or a role model.

Religion to unite

For some young people, being part of a religious group provides a sense of community and belonging. They feel less alone when navigating the world, facing moral dilemmas and making difficult decisions. Being connected to a 'higher power' or believing in God can also provide a sense of purpose and meaning. For others, practices such as praying, meditation and thanksgiving help them feel grounded, calm and centred in a chaotic world.

Studies show that having a religion can increase a person's resilience against the temptation to engage in unsafe behaviour, such as violence, stealing or taking drugs.

Religion can be a powerful force for good – bringing people together and helping the most vulnerable in society. The Civil Rights Movement in America was led by religious leaders, including Dr Martin Luther King Jr. and other activists from Black churches. Meetings were held in churches and money was raised for campaigns against racism and segregation.

Today, religious institutions are addressing the equality gap caused by failing governments, wars and natural disasters. Many religious institutions take up issues of social responsibility and tackle poverty, access to education and healthcare. Both religious and secular charities, such as Muslim Aid, the Red Cross, The Salvation Army and Médecins Sans Frontières, work in service of a better world.

Story time

As a Black woman, my faith brings me serenity and confidence. I remember growing up and often feeling like I was the ugly friend to my light-skinned and mixed-race friends. I would try to remind myself that, despite what other people say, I am made in the image of God, so I am beautifully and wonderfully made. Reminding myself that I am divine still gives me so much boldness.

"Being Hindu means knowing that God is everywhere and in everything and in me. As God does, I will also. That means loving all things and treating everything with respect."
Meera (13)

Religion to divide

For all the good of religion and its institutions, there are those who use it as a force for oppression, discrimination and control. For example, while I have found much peace and confidence in my faith, I also recognise that Christianity was used by European powers to justify slavery and colonise Africa. And even now, some churches refuse to give women the opportunity to preach, teach or take up leadership positions.

Being a girl in religious spaces can be liberating but also difficult to navigate. Some girls feel domesticated by religion; they are made to think that they can only aspire towards traditional roles in the household, such as homemaking or childbearing. As a result of this, some girls limit their potential or choose not to consider leadership roles out of fear that instructing men or speaking over them is wrong or sinful.

In moments like this, I think of incredible women like Reverend Rose Hudson-Wilkin, the first Black female bishop in Britain and personal chaplain to Queen Elizabeth II. Reverend Rose believed she was called to lead and serve in the Church but had to battle racism and sexism before she could take on positions of leadership. In my beliefs, I consider myself equal in worth, value and abilities to a man. It is okay to belong to a religion but disagree with certain rules or interpretations of sacred texts. We need more women like Rose in all sects of religion to champion inclusivity and belonging.

Extremism

Sometimes religious traditions can produce extremist movements. This happens when members of a religion feel their beliefs are superior to others. They may become intolerant and violent towards people from different faiths. Sadly, there are many examples of extremism across various religions.

In Myanmar, for many years Buddhist extremists have perpetrated violence towards Rohingya Muslims who are a minority group. In 2016, Buddhist extremists and the military forced 87,000 Rohingya to flee Myanmar. The extremists justified the persecution with arguments about Buddhism being under threat from other religions.

Al Qaeda and so-called 'Islamic State' are extremist groups that align themselves with Islam. They have carried out terror attacks around the world. It's important to note that their interpretation of Islam is rejected by most Muslims, who understand their religion to be one of peace.

Radicalisation

In 2015, three British teenagers from east London, Shamima Begum, Kadiza Sultana and Amira Abase, travelled to Syria to become members of the extremist group, ISIL (Islamic State of Iraq and the Levant). Shamima was radicalised by a school friend who had already left the UK for Syria. After ten days, she married an ISIL member. Shamima later appealed to the UK government, asking to return home to give birth to her son; she was refused and her British citizenship was revoked.

It is very important to remember that extremist groups in any religion do not represent the views or wishes of the majority of people who identify with the same religion.

Religious discrimination

People who openly share their faith are at risk of being targeted, discriminated against or even attacked for what they believe. Your religion may mean that you dress in a certain way – for example, some Muslim women might wear a hijab or burka, while some Sikh men wear turbans to cover their hair. Modest dressing or the practice of covering hair is sometimes assumed to be a sign of oppression or captivity. This is only true if a person is forced to comply with certain standards of dressing against their will. For many, the choice to follow a religious dress code is an important part of their identity.

Get to know some key terms that describe different forms of religious prejudice:

Religious persecution

The mistreatment of, oppression of or hostility towards a person or group of people based on their religious beliefs.

Islamophobia

The fear and hatred of Islam and Muslims. Muslims become the victims of Islamophobia when they are attacked purely because of their beliefs.

Antisemitism

Hostility, prejudice and discrimination against Jewish people.

"Hijab, to me, serves as a special little reminder that my body is my own and not for capital consumption."
Maryam

Doubts and questions

Maybe you were born into a religious family, but you find that your views, values and beliefs are changing. This does not have to mean that you are losing your faith or religion; it might instead be that your engagement with your faith is maturing. Having doubts can be helpful. They can help you to explore scriptures and other texts for yourself, seeking answers and carving out your own spiritual journey.

Faith or religion?

Sometimes doubts grow into a scepticism towards religion, and that's okay. Religion is defined as a belief system that structures the way you view the world, whereas faith is more of a personal, spiritual conviction. You can identify with spirituality and faith outside of religion, and it can still shape your morals, values and life decisions. For example, you may have heard of practices like meditation, mindfulness, acts of compassion or 'giving gratitude' – these activities feature in all five of the major religions but can also be practised in a secular (non-religious) sense.

> "Mindfulness helps us to live in harmony with our thoughts, words, and actions."
> *Amit Ray*

Speak up

If you're experiencing doubt or would like to start challenging aspects of your religion that feel harmful or unjust, then it is your right to start asking questions. They encourage transparency and honesty and will help you understand what you believe and why.

Sadly, there are some religious leaders who want to abuse their power and access to a congregation of people. It is important to speak up if something does not feel right. If a harmful practice is being encouraged at your temple, mosque, church, synagogue or wherever you worship, speak to an adult you trust. This could be a person outside of the religion, like a teacher, or one of the organisations at the back of this book.

Politics

What comes to mind when you read the word 'politics'? Maybe you think it is about giving people a voice. Maybe you think it's a dirty game played by the rich and privileged. The truth is, politics can be BOTH these things, but it is also so much more! Politics (and political systems) can sometimes be difficult to understand or just seem so detached from our everyday lives, realities and struggles. But politicians have the power to create laws and policies that can affect your present and future with things like access to healthcare, youth services, the price of university and the state of public transport. Politics is definitely worth understanding and even participating in.

Let's demystify politics

Politics is essentially the system through which the world is run but there are different governments and political systems across the globe.

Left-wing politics
Political beliefs based on the understanding that people should be equal to each other, regardless of race, gender or class.

Communism
Communists do not believe in the idea of private property; everything should be owned communally. Wealth should be shared equally by everyone.

Socialism
Socialists believe that all people are equal and that resources (including money) should be redistributed to address inequalities so that every member of society has a good quality of life.

Totalitarian
In this type of government, the leader tries to take total control of the lives of their citizens. There is no individual freedom. This form of governing was seen in Nazi Germany under Hitler's rule and is currently operating in North Korea under the Kim dynasty.

Democratic
The word 'democracy' comes from the Greek word 'demos' (people) and 'kratos' (power). The literal translation means 'rule of the people'. It is a political system that relies on freely given votes from citizens. They choose who the decision-makers will be.

Monarchic
In this political system, all the governing power resides with one family who rule from one generation to the next. Some royal families still rule today in Saudi Arabia, Cambodia, Luxembourg and Belgium. In the UK, the royal family holds a largely ceremonial role because the power to create laws and govern lies with the parliament.

Authoritarian
In this type of political system, power is placed in the hands of a leader or government that is not answerable to the people. This system opposes individual freedom because citizens do not get to elect or choose their leaders freely. Military dictatorships are an example of this system.

Right-wing politics
Political beliefs that focus on traditional cultures and values and economic freedom.

Liberalism
This belief is about protecting the rights of individual freedom. It holds that all civil liberties, such as the right to vote and freedom of speech, must be protected by the state.

Conservatism
This political belief is associated with socially traditional ideas, such as supporting the monarchy. It is typically opposed to rapid modernisation and values ideas and institutions such as the Church, the family and property ownership.

UK politics

In the UK, we have a democracy. This means that everyone over 18 shares in the right to vote. Within a democratic nation, certain basic rights are guaranteed, such as freedom of expression – anyone has the right to criticise and challenge the government openly. Many nations of the world are governed by totalitarian or authoritarian governments, under which people have sadly faced torture, execution or exile for speaking their mind and sharing critical opinions of leaders.

The party system

In the UK, the two main political parties are Labour and the Conservatives. They have been on opposing sides and battling it out in government since the start of the 20th century.

Conservative Party
The Conservatives historically have a focused interest in business and capitalism. They believe in private ownership, a strong military and upholding traditional values and institutions.

The Labour Party
It was founded in 1900 to promote the rights of working people. Labour believes that wealth and power should be shared more fairly and that public services should be free for everyone.

Liberal Democrats
This party sits between Labour and the Conservatives on the political spectrum. They encourage the creation of more businesses and believe doing so will achieve a more open society.

Although there are three dominant parties, many other smaller parties exist, supported by people all over the country. For example, the Green Party is passionate about creating a just and sustainable society. They also stand for animal rights, civil liberties and non-violence.

The United Kingdom is made up of four countries: England, Wales, Scotland and Northern Ireland. The British government (based in Westminster, London) has sovereign supremacy, meaning it has the power to make laws for the four nations of the UK. However, in the late 1990s, there was a move for UK parliament to 'devolve' its power to each of the four nations. This means that Scotland, Wales and Northern Ireland each have their own parliament with devolved power to create laws and deliver public services on a local level.

HOLYROOD, SCOTLAND

STORMONT, NORTHERN IRELAND

SENEDD, WALES

WESTMINSTER, ENGLAND
x

"A functioning, robust democracy requires a healthy, educated, participatory followership, and an educated, morally grounded leadership."

Chinua Achebe

Voting

Across the UK, in order to vote you must be 18 years of age, a citizen of Britain, the Commonwealth or the Republic of Ireland and you must be registered to vote in your constituency. Some parties in the UK, including Labour and the Green Party, want to drop the voting age to 16. However, the Conservatives do not support this.

Did you know that at the age of 16, you have the legal right to:

- Sign up for the army
- Get married and have a family (in Scotland)
- Work full-time if you've finished school and have a National Insurance number
- Change your name

Some people think that if 16-year-olds are deemed competent enough to make these big life decisions and fight for their country, they should also get a say in the politics of their nation and participate more actively in democracy. What do you think? Should the voting age be lowered from 18? If so, what age do you think is appropriate and why?

Become a change-agent

Even if you are under 18 and can't vote right now, there are still so many ways you can get involved in politics and use the power you have as a young person.

1.

Decide your political concerns

Sometimes it is assumed that young people don't care about politics. This is wrong! Young people have big political concerns and are determined to DO something about them. Studies show that these are some of the biggest issues for young people right now:

Cost of living – food poverty, living wage, transport
Health and wellbeing – improved access to mental health support
Environment – fighting climate change
Tackling discrimination and hate crimes – sexism, racism, ableism, xenophobia
Finding good jobs and work experience
Safety – knife crime, bullying

If you want to find out more about the political concerns of your peers, check out the UK Youth Parliament's survey Make Your Mark. It's the largest survey of young people in Europe. Visit www.byc.org.uk to find out more and add your voice to the conversation.

"It's important that people take action not just on the issues that one has direct experience of, but also to express solidarity with other people who may also be suffering, even when the experience is different. I'd encourage young people to make sure they're doing a mix of things that feel personally resonant and that are an expression of solidarity."
Jeremy Heimans

2. Find out about your local MPs

Find out who your local MP is and raise issues with them. They are elected to represent your interests and those of others in your area, and it is your right to ensure they understand what your concerns are. Visit **www.theyworkforyou.com/mps**, then enter your postcode and you'll find your MP. You can email them your concerns, and if you are up for a chat, you can even check for when they hold an 'advice surgery'. These are appointments they hold locally where any member of their constituency can speak to them face to face.

3. Get involved with youth organisations

There are many groups, such as UK Youth Parliament or Bite The Ballot, that centre young people's voices and concerns. If you're between 11 and 18 years old, you can stand to be elected as a member of Youth Parliament in your constituency. From there, you will find out the concerns and issues affecting young people in your area and represent their views to decision-makers. Whether you're interested in stopping further NHS cuts, reducing travel costs for public transport or want to challenge all forms of sexism, racism and discrimination – this is a place to have your views heard. Search **www.byc.org.uk/uk/uk-youth-parliament** to find out more.

4. Become an activist

Maybe you don't want to join a political party or get involved in the system of politics at all. You might be interested in changing the world from outside the system. Activism has always been a part of youth culture, but now activists are even younger, stronger and more determined. Don't let ANYONE make you feel like you're just a cute kid making some noise. Refuse to be patronised or dismissed. You can be a radical activist, determined to make changes in your community and your world. Don't let anyone quench that fire.

Inspirational figures

History is filled with stories about girls and women who took a stand against political bullies or destructive policies. Here are some young girls making big changes around the world:

Amal Azzudin

In 2005, 15-year-old Amal Azzudin started a campaign for her friend who had been removed from her home, detained and threatened with deportation. She teamed up with some friends and set up a campaign group called the Glasgow Girls to protest about how asylum seekers were being treated. Amal and her friends, Emma, Jennifer, Toni-Lee, Ewelina and Roza, started a petition that everyone in their school signed. They then submitted it to their local MP; he took it to Scottish Parliament and managed to get their friend released.

> "I was just a normal teenage girl but when Agnesa was taken, I remember thinking, 'I can't just sit down and do nothing. That could have been my family.'"
> — Amal Azzudin

Marley Dias

Marley Dias was just 11 years old when she campaigned to donate 1,000 books that featured Black girls as the main characters to schools. Marley was frustrated by the lack of Black characters in the books she was being given to read – she was "sick of reading about white boys and dogs." Marley started the book donation campaign #1000BlackGirlBooks and hit her goal nine times over. She made the Forbes 30 Under 30 and received a Smithsonian Magazine's American Ingenuity Award.

Political activism

History is being written every day, so join the long line of activists that have gone before you. Here are just some of the strategies you can take to champion your political beliefs:

Petitions

This is a gentle yet powerful way to start making noise about the things you care about. Petitions show decision-makers that there are many citizens who feel passionate about an issue. They allow people to easily contribute to a movement and heap pressure on politicians to act. **Change.org** is a popular website in the UK used for petitions. You could start your own or lend your voice by signing one.

TIPS FOR petition writing

Think about who you need to persuade, ask yourself whether a petition is the best way to reach them and mindmap how you will get a lot of people to sign.

Keep your petition simple, ask people to include their name and postcode as proof that they exist and include the deadline for signatures. This will help to eliminate the bots.

Marches

Marches are political demonstrations (also called monster meetings) where a group of people walk to protest about an issue they feel strongly about. Marches often capture the attention of the media and decision-makers. Are you aware of any recent or historic protests that have had a profound impact on society? If not, you could read about these movements and protests:

The suffragettes (1832–1929)
The Civil Rights Movement (1954–1968)
The March on Washington (1963)
Take Back the Night (1975)

Thinking about planning a protest? Great! Get clear on your goals by asking yourself the following questions:

- What is the reason behind the protest?
- What are you trying to achieve?
- Who is most likely to join in?
- Which decision-makers are you trying to influence?
- What's the best place and time to stage your protest? Could you join forces with a similar protest that's being planned?

TIPS FOR
planning a march

On the day, make sure a trusted adult can accompany you and remember to bring plenty of water and snacks.

In the UK, about a week before you intend to march, you will need to write to the police with the names and addresses of the organisers, the route you intend to take and the date and time of the march.

The freedom to be curious

An important part of understanding who you are and what shapes your identity is exploring your belief systems and worldview. In this chapter, we began by looking inwards and defining our personal values before turning outwards and looking at how morals can become laws. We then explored two very big belief systems: religion and politics. On your self-discovery journey, it is essential to be honest with yourself about what you think and why. Whenever you need it, this chapter is here to remind you that you have the freedom to be curious about the world. You get to ask "why?" and in doing so, develop the boldness to have both faith and doubts.

"Technology gives us **power**, but it does not and cannot tell us how to use that power. Thanks to technology, we can instantly **communicate** across the world, but it still doesn't help us know what to say."

Jonathan Sacks

Chapter 8
The Internet

Let's explore . . . the benefits and dangers of life online, cancel culture, spotting fake news and your digital footprint.

Life online is a world of endless possibilities, and so it is perhaps no surprise that the average teenager spends between 16 and 62 hours there every week. The online world can be a wild, wild place, and navigating its tricky terrain can be tiring, overwhelming and scary. There is the anxiety that can come from FOMO (fear of missing out) or the loneliness of seeing photos of events you weren't invited to. The internet can harbour stranger-creeps and predators but sometimes the danger can come from people you know. However, let's not forget the positives! The internet is one of the golden treasures of our time – a bridge between worlds, a social equaliser. Everyone can get involved – no matter who you are, where you live, what you look like or what you're interested in, you can carve out a space for yourself online.

There is so much positive power, learning and connection up for grabs on the internet, but it is also a place where we must safeguard our hearts and minds from content that can be harmful and damaging. In this chapter, we tackle all things 'online safety' together so that you can be empowered to engage with the digital world and reclaim it as your territory too!

> "We are all now connected by the internet, like neurons in a giant brain."
> Stephen Hawking

The benefits

Not to be dramatic, but living in a technological world has revolutionised everything! If you are reading this book, you probably do not realise just how much the world has changed, because you grew up after the revolution. Let's celebrate some of the major ways the internet has changed how we live.

Global friendships

For many people, real life can be hard, isolated and lonely. The internet has provided platforms where we can connect over shared interests, such as gaming, writing, music, films or social causes. If making friends in real life is difficult for you, the online world can be a great way to find 'your people'. Sometimes it's hard to show our true selves in real life, but online we can more comfortably explore different sides of ourselves.

Affirmation

When we make friends or find a community online, we can connect with people who affirm us. This affirmation could be related to things like lifestyle, religious beliefs, fashion sense, opinions or political views. People sometimes speak of affirmation and seeking validation as if it's a bad thing, but being affirmed is a valid human desire to feel welcomed and appreciated. However, this desire can become addictive. It is important to build your self-esteem by learning to like who you are without needing others to raise you up.

Learning made easy

Ever wondered how to create a gourmet meal out of everyday groceries, play the guitar or learn a new language? Online there are millions of tutorials and handy guides for just about any skill or area of interest. By watching a masterclass, taking a course or listening to an informative podcast, you can access the knowledge of an expert who has spent decades in their field. Thanks to the web, we can all access top knowledge at the click of a button.

Financial
Thanks to the internet, Gen Z and millennials are taking advantage of the earning power that comes with social media. Young people can become successful through activities like influencing or selling things on platforms such as Etsy or Depop. The internet is also where big artists like Justin Bieber, The Weeknd, Jack Harlow and Doja Cat were discovered on platforms like YouTube and Vine. The online world is a place where a fan-fiction lover like Anna Todd can write a story that goes viral and wins the hearts of over two billion readers.

The great equaliser
Groups who were previously silenced for reasons such as social class, limited resources or age can use social-media platforms to share their opinions, lead campaigns and hold powerful people to account. In online spaces, anyone can start a protest or campaign and join in with important conversations. Power is no longer in the hands of a select few, and the internet has been a great equaliser.

JOURNAL TIME
Loving life online

I am sure you can think of the many ways technology and the digital world have served you. It could be the entertainment or the super-speedy delivery of your favourite meal. Have a think and write down the top three things you love about life online.

The dangers

Okay, due protocol observed, the online world is a gold mine. We have given the internet and all things digital their flowers. But now we get to be honest about the challenges and dangers. Getting it wrong can have a massive impact on your life, so let's talk about what happens when the web becomes a wild, wild place.

Addiction

While being online can give us a community of friends and the acceptance we might not get in real life, an addiction to social media can become an issue. According to addiction expert Dr Anna Lembke, being on our phones and using digital media have made many of us dopamine junkies. In Chapter 5, we discussed dopamine as being one of our 'feel-good' hormones, linked to rewards.

Dr Lembke tells us that dopamine hits come from various sources: the number of likes, the filter-enhanced faces and aesthetics and the algorithms constantly suggesting new posts, people and trends to binge. While we're scrolling, we feel great but once we stop, our dopamine levels plummet.

One of the ways to manage phone addiction is to go on a digital detox and take some time away from your mobile. It could be a day, a week or a month, but Dr Lembke advises that for those really addicted to socials, a month or longer is required. You can use apps to track your digital usage and set time limits. Another option is to put your phone on 'do not disturb' during certain hours or turn off your notifications. This can help you regain power and control. Stay tuned as we discuss more about how to digitally detox later on in this chapter.

Online but left out

Technology can bring people together and also tear them apart. While being addicted to online validation poses problems, on the flip side, online rejection can happen when you don't get what you are looking for. This can lead to feelings of alienation and a loss of self-esteem.

Studies have linked heavy social media use to loneliness, especially when the motive for being online is avoiding difficult feelings and situations in real life. During the Covid-19 pandemic, everyone was instructed to socially distance and schools, work, restaurants and transportation were all locked down. It was an isolating time for many and people turned to various social platforms to keep in touch and discover new connections. Ironically, more social media usage led to increased feelings of loneliness. We are currently suffering a loneliness epidemic, with young people and the elderly most affected.

The virtual world allows us to connect, but it does not replace the need for emotional connection. Many people are socially connected and emotionally alone. This is because you can't substitute large followings on social media for genuine friendships. It's healthy to question whether social media platforms and technology help lonely people or take advantage of their situation.

Cyberbullies

Bullying describes any unwanted behaviour that causes distress or harm. Cyberbullying happens online or with the use of technology. No one should ever have to tolerate any form of bullying, whether it's a one-off incident or persists over many years.

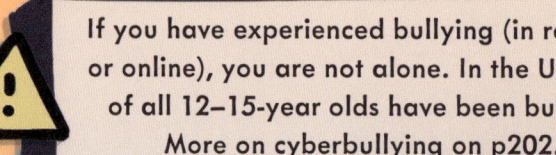

If you have experienced bullying (in real life or online), you are not alone. In the UK, half of all 12–15-year olds have been bullied. More on cyberbullying on p202.

Digital detox

We know the online world is addictive – the rush of dopamine from all the likes, comments and pretty pictures or videos we see. This feels good in the moment, but the withdrawal once we come offline can really affect our mind, mood and feelings. Being online can be an emotional roller coaster of comparison, consumerism (constantly buying stuff) and different opinions.

It is important to know when to log off and take a break. Various studies have found that limiting your time online can reduce feelings of loneliness, anxiety and depression (for young people *and* adults).

On the right are some signs that you may need to detox from the digital world and re-connect with yourself.

> Are you finding it hard to get enough sleep because you are up late checking your phone, watching reels, videos or responding to messages?
>
> Are you feeling unhappy and dissatisfied with your own life because of how great everyone else's life seems?
>
> Are you obsessing over how you look?
>
> Do you struggle to enjoy things without posting about them first?
>
> Do you get nervous or fidgety if you have not been able to check your notifications?
>
> Do you end up scrolling on social media without even realising it?
>
> Is social media the first thing you look at in the morning and the last thing at night?
>
> Are you getting in trouble with your parents or at school because of how much time you spend on your phone?
>
> Today 02:00

How to digital detox

- Start to follow meaningful accounts that make you happy.
- Unfollow accounts that make you question your self-worth.
- Come off social media for a month or three.
- Make a pledge with your friends not to use filters on your pictures.
- Limit daily screen time.

Everyone is different, so your digital detox will be personal to you.

Story time

14-year-old Lydia absolutely loved being on Snapchat because she felt able to be her free, fun self. She never had to overthink anything, posting in real time about what she was doing, eating and feeling.

One day, Lydia started receiving messages from an anonymous user who made cruel comments. Initially she ignored the messages. But then the person started sending them every day, sometimes several times a day, and each message was more malicious and hurtful than the last. This went on for a long time. The mean messages disappeared after a day, so Lydia tried telling herself it did not matter, but she started to feel really anxious whenever her notifications pinged.

The user then started telling Lydia to harm herself and send proof. When she refused to respond, they sent pictures of her hanging out with her friends after school, making it clear that they knew Lydia in real life. She started to feel scared, and she stopped going outside because she had no clue who the bully was and felt afraid they would harm her.

Thankfully, Lydia spoke to her family and friends and her mum challenged the school to start an investigation. Lydia began screenshotting the cruel messages and told the cyberbully she would share them with the school as part of their investigation. The person got scared, backed off and stopped contacting her.

REFLECTION

- What do you think was happening to Lydia?
- If you were her friend, what might the signs have been that something or someone was upsetting her?
- Lydia never responded to the taunts; why was this a powerful decision?
- Why was it important that she shared her online experience with her friends and mum?

Cancel culture

Remember how we celebrated the internet for being a great equaliser and giving power to people to speak their truth? Well, what happens when your views are different to everyone else's? What happens when your online community rejects you for speaking out? What happens when you are passionate about a social issue but do not know all the facts and get something wrong? Unfortunately, the answer to these questions is that you run the risk of being 'cancelled' online. A person gets cancelled when they are rejected or shamed by people and lose support.

'Cancelling' is a powerful tool in the court of social media and public opinion. It can be a way to hold people, businesses and even industries to account for harmful actions like racism or sexism. In 2016, activist April Reign created the #OscarsSoWhite campaign, and some celebrities chose to boycott or 'cancel' the awards because of the lack of diversity in its nominations. By 2021, many more people of colour were nominated for Oscars. So there's no doubt in this case that cancel culture worked in forcing the Oscars to do better.

But should we put the same amount of pressure and consequence on cancelling people who are still growing in their knowledge, beliefs and identities? Cancel culture can hamper diversity of thought and prevent us from having real dialogue about important issues.

Being rejected by friends can feel like the worst possible punishment. So it is no surprise that being cancelled and publicly shamed has been linked to suicidal thoughts, depression and anxiety. Studies show that even when young people care deeply about an issue and want to lend their voice in activism, they clam up in fear that they 'don't know enough to speak up' and will be judged online for getting the facts wrong.

Dealing with cancel culture

The point is, you should not have to become an expert or be absolutely perfect to talk about an issue you care about. Perhaps instead of **'cancelling'** a person, we can **'call out'** what they may have said or done wrong and give them an opportunity to think, apologise and change instead of condemning them.

Media psychologist Dr Don Grant suggests that to manage the dangers of cancel culture, everyone should practise **'good digital citizenship'**, which means thinking twice before posting on social media and trying not to engage in conversation when you are emotional. If you are the one doing the cancelling, it is important that you are honest with yourself. Do you cancel others to feel powerful, in control and like a leader? Is it something you do to build your self-esteem?

Try to nurture a healthy and authentic connection with yourself. It will feed into how you connect with other people. If your self-esteem and confidence is built by dragging others down, then you are walking in hostility instead of light and truth, and you deserve so much better than that.

Fake news
(and how to spot it)

Whether you are a budding activist in search of persuasive information to include in your campaign or you simply want to be in the loop with what's happening in the world, fake news can be a menace to deal with. It's sometimes difficult to tell the difference between fake news and reliable sources, and this is one of the things that makes the online sphere a tricky place to navigate. Fake news is dangerous and, in some cases, can be the difference between life and death. Unfortunate examples of this include an incident in Brazil where there was an outbreak of yellow fever. Following the outbreak, people claiming to be doctors spread misinformation on WhatsApp and discouraged people from taking the vaccine.

Back in the day, we got our news from good old-fashioned print media sources, like newspapers, magazines and books, which generally went through a rigorous process of being checked, analysed and critiqued for inaccuracies. Newspapers can still be biased and editors and journalists may have to skew their reporting to align with the interests of newspaper owners, but the internet has had a profound impact on journalism and has changed how we deliver and read the news.

Nowadays, anyone can make something up, write it down and share it, wreaking havoc. Due to savvy, snooping algorithms, the internet will also give you more of what you search for or consume. When it comes to news and information, it is easy for the online space to become an echo chamber of your own opinions, right or wrong. Knowing this, it is important to seek a range of views.

QUESTION THE STORY

Whether you are reading a news story in a well-known newspaper or on a blog, website or social media feed, keep the following in mind:

The who – who is behind this story? Are they credible and trustworthy? Is there a shady URL ending in '.lo' or '.com.co'?

The why – why was this story written? Does the author have an agenda for distorting the facts? Why was this story sent to you?

Compare – check websites like **factcheck.org** or reputable news sources to see if the claims being made are backed up.

Get critical – are the statistics and figures reliable? What are the story's sources? Is the information exaggerated in any way? Are the words or language a form of clickbait to shock you into reading on? Are there spelling mistakes, invalid dates or language that is not news-like?

It is important for you to become a critical consumer of online information. Having these points in mind will ensure you are taking an analytical approach to news reading. Journalists have a trick called 'triangulation' – if you are able to find at least three credible, separate sources that back up a statement or piece of news, then it is likely to be factual and not fake news.

When the news (fake or real) about global issues gets too much, remember that you can switch off. This does not mean you don't care; it means you have prioritised your wellbeing and mental health.

Your digital footprint

There are benefits and dangers to being online. But you do not have to disengage from the web completely to stay safe. There are ways you can reclaim the online world and remain empowered as you enjoy the benefits of digital connection.

An active digital footprint is one you intentionally leave through your posts on social media or blog posts. You are actively creating a digital footprint when you share information about yourself. This could be through writing a post on social media, completing an online form, signing up to a newsletter or accepting cookies on your browser.

The data trail

Everyone leaves behind a digital footprint, whether they know it or not. It's the trail of data you create while using the internet. It comes from your social media posts, searches, saved passwords, online purchases and IP addresses.

A passive digital footprint builds without you knowing. It is created from your use of apps and websites that ask for your location. It also comes from online shopping, products you browse and reviews you watch, which allow big companies to send you targeted adverts. It is passive because you are not actively writing posts, commenting or even sharing but it is the result of your movement online.

Employers and universities can use search engines to screen applicants and look at their social media, and having a bad digital footprint can be very costly. One group of teenagers had their Harvard University admission offers taken away after they were caught sharing racist and offensive memes in a Facebook group. Check your digital footprint by typing your name into a search engine. Pay attention to the posts, comments and images that come up.

Protecting yourself online

- Address any issues or problematic comments that come up when you search your name. Delete the posts if you can. If you can't, then contact the site owner and ask them to delete your comment.
- Use a separate email address or nickname for personal social media accounts.
- Secure your privacy settings on social media (see the suggestions above).
- Be responsible and mindful of what you share online.
- Do not visit websites that make you nervous or uncomfortable.

Tame the wild, wild web

Life online is exciting, and in this chapter we've looked at some of the benefits – making global friendships, finding a great community, learning new skills and even having your talents discovered. We have also been real about the drawbacks. There are ways to avoid these landmines though once we learn to navigate addiction, cope with rejection, deal with trolls and spot fake news.

You can be totally empowered to reclaim the web as a safe space and enjoy the benefits of being digitally connected. And if it all gets too much, you can pull the plug. You have the POWER to sign out of that world, centre yourself and enjoy the beautiful things life has to offer. Despite all the 'connecting' that is going on digitally, there is also an epidemic of loneliness and isolation. This is because being on social media is not the same as spending time with people, in real life, face to face. When being online gets too much, remember you can take your passions offline. Take time to remember all the things you enjoy doing outside of being online and have fun doing them.

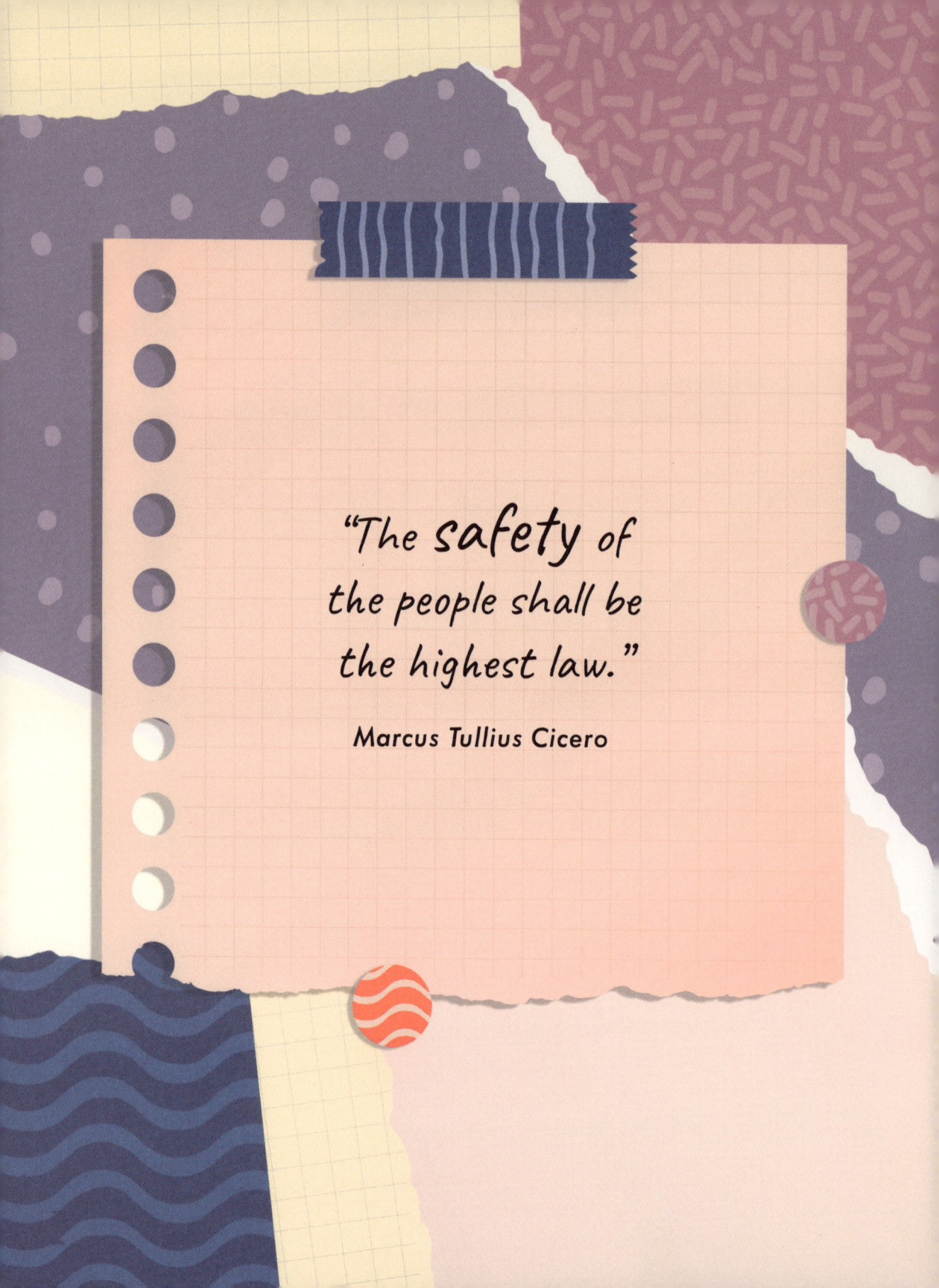

"The **safety** of the people shall be the highest law."

Marcus Tullius Cicero

Chapter 9
Your Safety

Let's explore... relationship safety, victim blaming, crime, cultural safety, online safety and protecting yourself.

This chapter covers topics that some readers may find difficult or upsetting. It is totally fine if you don't feel ready to explore these themes. You can skip to page 204 and come back to this part of the book whenever you like.

In all things, your safety comes first and this is the common thread weaving together all the different topics in this book. Whether you're thinking about your friendship circles, life at home, showing up as your authentic self at school or on your favourite apps, understanding what is safe and healthy, while calling out anyone or anything that puts you at risk, is super important. Whichever way you choose to navigate the world, feeling safe in your mind and body is your right.

In this chapter, we revisit some of the topics we have already discussed but place an emphasis on your safety. While some of the issues in this chapter may not relate to you, reading through them can still equip you with the language to support a friend who might be in an unsafe situation.

Relationship safety

Toxic relationships

Toxic, abusive or violent relationships can happen to anyone; it does not matter their age, race, gender or background. Some grown-ups make the mistake of thinking only adult relationships can be controlling and abusive, but that is a big myth – relationships between young people can also result in harm and abuse. A study by the NSPCC, a leading UK children's charity, found that a quarter of girls aged 13 to 17 experienced physical violence or emotional abuse in their relationships.

We need to be prepared to listen to anyone who has concerns about their relationship, no matter their age. This may not apply to you, but it is important to watch out for toxic relationships among friends and family members too.

Activity time: *It's giving toxic*

Have a look at the scenarios in the speech bubbles. Which of them do you have concerns about and why?

"Why are you wearing that? Are you trying to get other guys to look at you?"

"Are you really going to eat that? You've gained weight . . . might be better if you skip a meal – just looking out for you."

"I had my friends catfish you – I just had to make sure you were not cheating on me."

"I am only checking your phone because I want this relationship to work."

Some of the quotes above could look like someone displaying care or being protective, but actually these are the signs of control and abuse. Abuse is not always physical. Coercive control can include threats, humiliation or intimidation used to harm, punish or isolate victims. It is a criminal offence in the UK. If something like this happens to you, it is not your fault and you should speak to a trusted adult.

Victim blaming and shaming

Victim blaming and shaming happen when a victim of abuse, crime or any wrongful act is considered entirely or partially to blame for the harm and then shamed for it. For example, a girl might be stalked and harassed by someone but then told that she deserved it because of her clothing choices.

So many girls and women experience shame, trauma and humiliation when they dare to speak up about their experiences of abuse, especially against powerful men. This is why the global #MeToo movement was so revolutionary. It was a campaign started by Tarana Burke back in 2006 to give a voice to victims of violence and abuse.

In 2017, #MeToo went viral after it was used by several women who had been sexually abused by Harvey Weinstein, a powerful Hollywood producer. These survivors stood up to Weinstein and refused to be blamed, shamed or silenced. They sparked change in society, the law and workplace policies around violence and harassment.

Speaking out

Speaking out about an abusive and toxic relationship can be hard. In many ways, as a society we are getting better at listening to victims of abuse and giving them the space to share their stories and lead with their experiences. However, negative attitudes still persist.

Past experiences

Some people experience abuse at very young ages, when they won't be able to safely stand up for themselves or understand they have the right to say no. This isn't their fault, nor should they feel ashamed by what's happened. In these situations, it is always best to speak to a trusted adult to get help.

Even though these issues affect girls hugely, it is also hard for boys and men to speak out sometimes because of false assumptions that men are not vulnerable to abuse.

Activity time: *Say no to victim blaming*

Look at these common examples of victim blaming and shaming. Why do you think victims are sometimes ignored or disbelieved?

"Why didn't you scream for help?"

"You must have sent mixed messages."

"What were you doing there anyway?"

"Why did it take you so long to say something?"

Story time

I wish my younger self had fully understood that my body belonged to me, that it was sacred and special. Time and time again, I would find my personal and physical boundaries being challenged and interfered with by complete strangers. I could be in Lidl buying a croissant or on the bus going home from school, and I would find myself being approached by strange men trying to get my number. It was not flattering. Many of them would become rude and hostile if I ignored their advances.

One time, I was on a coach to London and one of the male passengers initially complimented my hair (which was out in an afro). I thanked him, found my seat and put my headphones in. I wasn't listening to any music, but I had made it a strategy to avoid eye-contact and conversation with men in public. He tried to engage me in conversation and, like many other men before, became verbally violent and began swearing at me for ignoring him.

For a long time, the coach was absolutely silent, everyone minding their own business — no one wanting

REFLECTION

I have since learned that my body and personal space are mine. They did not belong to the creepy older men who whistled, shouted or stared at my bum. My body was not the property of teenage boys or drunk men on coaches.

to get involved. I still had my headphones in and kept acting like I couldn't hear him, which infuriated him further. Eventually, an older female passenger told him to back off and he turned his viciousness towards her.

It was a horrible experience. The British Transport Police were called to the coach station when we arrived, but at that point I did not want to speak to anyone. I just wanted to go home and forget the whole ordeal. In truth, I could never forget and I wish I had reported him for harassing me.

My body exists for **me**. It is my **home**, and my **safe place** and I have **every right** to stand in **defence of it**.

Crime and safety

The 'S' word – snitching or speaking up?

There are times when safety conflicts with other values, like protecting a friend by not telling on them and being seen as a 'snitch'. Being accused of 'snitching' or 'snaking' can feel like the end of the world. It hurts to feel like everyone's on edge around you, that no one tells you anything any more because you 'told' on someone that one time. You are faced with the moral dilemma – do I speak up or stay silent?

There are ways to safely speak up without endangering yourself or exposing your identity. For more information on how to report crime anonymously, check out: **fearless.org**. You can report via their website (it scrambles IP addresses so your device cannot be tracked or traced).

There might be times when someone says, "Don't tell" or "Let's keep this a secret", but what they are really asking is that you cover up your own or someone else's suffering. You owe bullies and abusers NOTHING – whether they are children, adults, friends or strangers. I know this is hard to accept; I have had conversations with thousands of young people who felt ashamed or were worried about upsetting someone or being called a snitch. I understood their concerns but challenged them to think of situations where speaking up, especially about crime and safety, could be the difference between life and death.

When home is not safe

There are many pretty quotes about family life, such as:

> "There is no place like home."

While this should always be the case, and is for many people, some may find themselves in a family where they feel unsafe, unloved and uncared for. This is different to imperfect people messily trying to figure out how to 'do family' together. An unsafe home should not be tolerated. As a young person, your needs and safety come first (and this is according to law).

No harm will be tolerated!

Sometimes money issues, mental health challenges or drug and alcohol addiction can make parents unable to look out for their children. Sometimes harms can happen outside of home without your parents knowing or being able to support you. Here are some examples of abuse or neglect:

Emotional abuse damages a person's self-worth and harms their emotional wellbeing. It can take many forms, but some signs include threats, humiliation, manipulation, name-calling or a lack of warmth and support.

Child neglect happens when a parent fails to meet a child's basic needs. This is the most common form of abuse in the UK. Signs of neglect include being left hungry, dirty or without clean clothes, or not being taken to the doctor's when you need medical support.

Physical abuse happens when a young person is hurt on purpose. In some cultures, physical discipline is quite common and children might get 'beats' or 'licks' when they do something wrong, or they might be made to hold uncomfortable positions as a punishment. However, in the UK physical punishments like this are not tolerated and in some situations are against the law.

Domestic abuse occurs when one parent is being physically or emotionally abusive towards the other. Being exposed to this or witnessing it as a child is also a form of abuse. It can negatively affect your wellbeing and make home feel unsafe.

Online abuse happens when a person sends mean messages or threats using a phone or computer. Online abuse also includes stalking on social media, hacking accounts and monitoring messages and call logs.

Sexual abuse is when a young person is persuaded, forced or tricked into sexual activities. Sexual abuse can involve someone touching you sexually, making you undress or persuading you to touch someone else. Sexual abuse doesn't have to involve touching: if someone makes you look at porn, watch them undress or pose for sexual pictures, it is also abuse. Sexual abuse can be very confusing and hard to identify, but if anything has made you feel worried, it is always a good idea to speak to a trusted adult, like your school safeguarding lead. They are trained to know what to do when you come to them with worries like this. Remember, sexual abuse is never your fault, and it is important to speak up to make sure you are kept safe, even if the abuse happened long ago.

Grooming is when someone older, but not necessarily an adult, builds a relationship with a young person to gain their trust, so they can manipulate or exploit them. Exploitation is when a person is being used or treated unfairly to benefit another person. Sometimes grooming can start with gift giving. This can make you feel special and cared for but also indebted, as though you owe the groomer. From gift giving, grooming can progress to being asked to keep secrets, being threatened, being isolated and receiving sexual messages or images. A groomer can be anyone – a stranger, family member or friend. Child grooming is still abuse even if the adult has not touched the child physically. Grooming can also lead to the other forms of abuse listed previously.

Financial abuse occurs when someone demands control over your money and how you spend it or tries to prevent you from earning your own money.

Sadly, harm can come from within the home and from outside it. But remember, it is not your responsibility to parent yourself or your parents. You do not have to take on their struggles and problems and you do not have to suffer in silence. You can speak to a teacher about how you are feeling. If you are not sure which teacher to talk to, every school has a pastoral care or wellbeing team, who you can open up to about your feelings and what's going on for you, whether at home or outside it. You could also speak to your GP or call an anonymous helpline. See the resources section for numbers to call.

Remember that witnessing any of these forms of abuse still counts as abuse itself. Lots of young people worry that if they speak up, social workers will take them away from their parents. This happens rarely as the main goal is to help your parents support you.

This section may not affect you personally, but it is important to be aware of these issues, as you may spot the signs of abuse or neglect in friends. There are different signs that a person is being abused, hurt or groomed. Here are a few to keep in mind: a person becoming withdrawn and isolating themselves from friends and family, suddenly changing their normal habits, having gifts they cannot explain, being secretive, using sexual language or going missing from home and school.

Safety within cultures

Cultural harms

No two families are the same. We all have quirks and strange ways of doing things. It could be your dad's special way of making the Sunday roast or maybe your grandma adds vegetables to her jollof rice. Every family has its own rituals and traditions, which may be cultural, religious or unique to them. But let's be very clear – absolutely no one is ever allowed to justify causing harm, distress or pain on the grounds of culture, religion or family traditions.

Forced marriage, honour-based violence and female genital mutilation are violent practices that can happen within families. They are hidden crimes because they tend to go on behind closed doors. Some parents may try to justify these harms on so-called cultural grounds, but these acts violate human rights and are unjustifiable and illegal. Your family may not condone these behaviours, but it is important to know about them because your awareness and ability to spot the signs could greatly help someone else.

Female genital mutilation

happens when a girl's genitals are cut, altered or removed. This can happen when a girl is born, during childhood, adolescence or even as an adult. It is a form of physical and sexual abuse that happens within families and is falsely justified on cultural and religious grounds. Female genital mutilation is illegal even if it happens outside the UK, and there is a special police unit who work to protect girls from it.

(So-called) honour-based violence

can happen to children or adults who are believed to have brought disgrace to the family. As a result, they are subjected to harm and abuse. There is never honour in abusing another person.

Forced marriage

occurs when a person is made to marry someone against their consent.

Online safety

Governments are beginning to realise that society cannot simply keep young people safe by telling them to 'stay offline'; it is unfair and impractical. Many now recognise that they need to step up their commitment to protecting people from illegal and harmful online activity. The UK government has introduced an online safety bill that places regulations on social media companies and makes them legally responsible for the content they host, forcing them to put protections in place to safeguard people. The existence of this important bill emphasises the need for technology companies to step up, make safety part of their design and do more to protect young people online.

Is social media for you?

The minimum age for most platforms is 13 years old, but some apps have a higher age requirement. Many people lie about their age to access social media. But lying to access something means you are probably exposing yourself to more harm than fun . . .

Sharing is revealing

Sharing online can be totally fine (and fun). Relive your fabulous day out, share pictures of the fancy dessert or beautiful cupcake you had at lunch – spread the love, share the joy, why not! But remember that your pictures, comments and videos are seen and read by more people than you know.

There might be times you are feeling down in the dumps; you might want to let people know how very sad you are. But stop – really think before you share. Yes, we are living in a time of #authenticity, and it's okay to not be okay, but be honest about why you want to post a vulnerable moment. Is it that you want sympathy? Is validation addiction stirring up again? No shame if that's what you want – love and attention are basic human desires – but it might be healthier to speak to a friend, parent, mentor or teacher instead to avoid unwanted comments and ensure that you are affirmed by someone who truly loves or cares about you.

If you ever feel livid, hurt or betrayed, you could take a moment to pause and find a healthy way to let those emotions out instead of ranting away on your timeline. Revisit the wheel of emotions in Chapter 5 and use some of the techniques discussed to blow off steam. Before you share online, remember that even if you take down the post, you can't erase it from the minds of the people who have seen it.

Sexting

Sexting is when people share sexual messages, videos or pictures with another person. In the UK, sexting is illegal for all under the age of 18. Although the laws around sexting were originally designed to catch paedophiles who had indecent pictures of children, young people can be criminalised for sending pictures of themselves.

If anyone is pressuring you to send intimate pictures that you would not be comfortable with Grandma seeing, say no and BLOCK them. You can use apps, like ZIPIT (created by Childline), which give you a funny way to say NO. Once a picture is out there, you have no control over how far it goes; you may think you are sending it to just one person, but they then have the power to pass it on to as many people as they want. Do not give ANYONE that hold over you.

Easy with the selfies

We all love a good selfie, but is your new profile picture showing more than it should? Yes, you want to personalise your blog, social media or biography on a gaming site and you totally should. But stop to think about whether your selfie (and any other picture you post) is giving too much away – for instance, where you go to school, where you live or where you and your friends hang out.

You might think your page is on private and so you've screened out strangers, but what about the friends of your friends? They might not be strangers to your bestie but they are to you. Someone could get access to these pictures and use them as a way to track you.

Always take care and, if in doubt, don't use a selfie as your display picture; you could use a picture of your pet or favourite animal instead. It is wise to have a trusted adult look at the image and screen it for giving away any personal clues before you put it up.

HOW TO
create online boundaries

Establishing personal boundaries online is really important. While it's great that you can meet new people and make friends on the Internet, you never really and truly know who they are. Here are some ways to create online boundaries.

Use a nickname
Avoid using your full name online and do not give out personal details.

Is your location visible?
Apps are always asking whether they can put location settings on. This gives satellites permission to pick up your exact location. Mindlessly we often click 'yes' but are you aware of what you are consenting to? Family and friends can see where you are but so can everyone else, including cyberbullies, stalkers and trolls.

Think before meeting an online friend
Never EVER go and meet up with someone you have met online without a trusted adult. (No one is trying to baby you; this is sound advice for adults as well.) Make sure you meet in public spaces. If an online friend only wants to meet up in private, know that this is a RED FLAG and they might have another agenda.

Check your privacy settings
This is like closing the curtains to make sure nosy neighbours cannot peer into your house. Make sure that your posts are only visible to friends. People can still send you 'friend' or 'follow' requests, but you get to choose who watches, sees or reads your online content.

Cyberbullying

Cyberbullies use various tools including laptops, recording devices, gaming platforms and social media. Examples of cyberbullying include:

Trolling
Causing conflict, hostility and arguments online with offensive messages or personal attacks.

Online stalking
Sending repeated or threatening messages of harassment or hacking into online accounts.

Online grooming
This is when people are manipulated and pressured online into doing things they don't want to do. The NSPCC found that online grooming has risen by 80% since 2019. Recent data shows that Snapchat is the most used platform for child-grooming.

Spreading abusive rumours, gossip and lies online.

Posting private information without consent.

Things to remember

You are not the problem
Bullying (in any form) is not your fault. The fault lies completely with the bully. Do not waste your precious energy trying to understand why the bullies chose to pick on you; that is not your responsibility.

The block button is your friend
The cyberbully, stalker or troll wants you to engage. Do not take the bait. Never agree to meet in person to confront their behaviour; this person is dangerous and cannot be trusted. Immediately block anyone who makes you feel unsafe or uncomfortable online.

Document everything
Take screenshots or print things out. This is proof of the bullying and helpful for the school, police or social media platforms you may report to.

It is never too late to back out
We've all made mistakes online. Maybe you accepted a friend request from a stranger who started off friendly but is now pressuring you to do video chats or send nude pictures. You might want to blame yourself or think you are in too deep to back out. But you are the victim and they are the abuser. You can always change your mind, even if you have said yes before.

Tell an adult that you trust
It might seem awkward to tell someone about the bullying or show them the messages or images you are being sent if they feel embarrassing. But you do not have to go through this alone. Speaking to an adult can help, especially if you decide to report it to the police.

REFLECTION

We have covered a lot of tough topics in this chapter. Take some time to think over and reflect on what you have read. Feel free to write down anything that might have confused or worried you. It could be helpful and reassuring to speak to a trusted adult about any concerns you might have.

Protecting yourself

I am aware that this chapter took a heavy turn and that some of you will not relate to the sad situations we have discussed. However, I hope this information will help you to empathise (grow in sympathy and understanding) with others who may be affected by abuse. If you have questions or concerns about any of the issues raised, it is really important that you speak to a trusted adult or call one of the helplines listed in the resource section. This book is here to raise awareness and ensure that you are better informed. But it is the trusted people in your life who will support you if you choose to take ACTION.

"The choices we make today create the future that we are dreaming of."

Kapil Tetarwal

Chapter 10
Future You

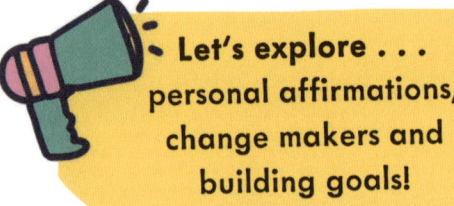

Let's explore... personal affirmations, change makers and building goals!

An ode to the person you are becoming

The purpose of this book has been exploring, celebrating and challenging all the wonderful aspects that make up YOU. We have covered a ton of important topics, from identifying your beliefs and values to building your identity and exploring how to have a healthy relationship with yourself, your friends and your family. This may be the last chapter in the book, but it marks the beginning of your bold journey, now armed with a deeper knowledge and love of yourself. This chapter is an ode to the brave human you are becoming.

Dreaming big can feel scary. You might wonder, "What if my dreams do not come true? What if I share my ideas and nothing comes of them?" But being brave is not about having everything figured out. Being brave is trying your best – it's laughing at yourself when you get it wrong, learning from your mistakes and changing direction. A brave person does not think little of themselves, their life and their future. They have reclaimed their power from the jaws of fear, and they are willing to bet on themselves again and again.

This is your life. Be brave enough to take a chance on you. Don't overthink it; let your curiosity lead you to open doors. Pick up that pencil and start sketching. Open up the computer or notebook and start drafting your novel. Pick up your phone and start recording your video or podcast. However you want to impact the world around you, just go for it! Start small and watch your wildest dreams unfold. Give yourself permission to believe that wonderful, audacious things are possible for you.

> "Don't let anyone rob you of your imagination, your creativity, or your curiosity. It's your place in the world; it's your life. Go on and do all you can with it, and make it the life you want to live."
>
> Mae Jemison

Story time

When I started studying at Oxford University, I remember feeling so unsure of myself. Despite having a first-class law degree and a strong CV, progressing through a competitive admissions process and securing a scholarship, I arrived at the Oxford Law Faculty feeling like an imposter. The fancy titles for the different semesters, saying Latin grace at traditional dinners, wearing gowns to sit exams and the gruelling rigour of the course were all too much. I spent the first few months trying (unsuccessfully) to hide and trying to just focus on getting through it. But then I realised that hiding and merely surviving simply would not do. I had to make my being there count for something. I thought hard about how I could help improve access for others who might be considering Oxford or Cambridge. I decided to organise an interactive law access day at my college (Wadham) and invited students from my former secondary school and sixth-form college.

I pitched the idea to my college advisor and the access team at Wadham College. Everyone was keen but wondered how I would convince busy barristers and senior judges to come and conduct workshops with students. I approached my mentors at the Kalisher Trust, the charity sponsoring my scholarship, and they enthusiastically provided a list of legal practitioners available to attend the event and conduct workshops. Everything came together; the students received application and personal statement advice, and they also had direct access to barristers and senior judges and were able to ask questions and develop their confidence.

This experience taught me a valuable lesson – instead of focusing my energy on shrinking when I find myself in an uncomfortable space, there is so much more power in taking ownership of the access, opportunity and privilege that space provides and opening the gate for someone else.

Affirmations

Always affirm yourself. Affirmations have the power to help you focus on what matters and change negative thought patterns. By practising self-affirmations, you are reminding yourself daily that you are capable, strong and worthy. Affirmations are statements you can say aloud to yourself every day or write down somewhere you will see them.

Here are some positive affirmations to start you off:

> "You are your best thing."
> Toni Morrison

- I can do this.
- I am confident.
- I learn from my mistakes.
- Today, I am open to new opportunities and experiences.
- My smile is my gift to the world.
- I do not let my fear hold me back.
- Good things happen to me.
- I choose to let go of the old and embrace the new things today brings.
- I have the power to change my story.

JOURNAL TIME

Affirming yourself

Write out five affirmations personal to you.

Future you

What a time to be alive, with so much inspiration, courage and elevation in the world. You stand tall among countless people finding their brave, attempting difficult things and doing their bit to shake up the world. We are all unique and have different access to opportunities, resources, platforms and privileges. But if we share the motivation, desire and passion to make our world a better place, we can start wherever we are, use the access we have and push for change. Just by reading this book, you have started to explore how much power, value and ability you have to offer. You bring so much to this world.

REFLECTION

Think about how you will use YOUR power to bring about change.

What do you think needs transformation in our world or culture?

What can you do today (even if it's just a small action) to move towards that goal?

Activity time
Write a letter to your future self

Write a letter to yourself which you can put in your journal or diary and revisit as time goes by or open in five years' time if you like. In this letter you can make predictions, envision the future and set goals for yourself. Some examples:

"Dear future me, spend quality time with friends and family and don't get too bogged down with life's difficulties."
Lilly (12)

"Dear future me, I hope your dreams come true. I hope you come out of your shell, overcome your fears and find happiness. Never let anyone bring you down."
Taria (12)

"Dear future me, how does it feel to have won the Nobel Prize in Literature? I hope your love for telling great stories continues to grow. You should be so proud of yourself."
Bukky (13)

Change makers

There are countless examples of normal girls who decided to be change makers. These girls had a vision for their world, became inspired to stand up for what they believed, developed a strategy and took action.

For **Malala Yousafzai**, it was simply doing what so many others take for granted – showing up to school – despite the threats against her life. When she was 11 years old, Malala wrote an anonymous blog for the BBC about her experience living under Taliban military rule in Pakistan. During this time, girls were not allowed to go to school in Pakistan. In her blog, Malala advocated for girls' right to education. In October 2012, Malala was shot by a Taliban gunman. This attempt against her life sparked an international movement to support her. When the Taliban threatened to attack her again, Malala fled to the UK with her family, where she continued her activism and founded the charity Malala Fund. In 2014, Malala became the youngest person to win the Nobel Peace Prize.

For **Greta Thunberg**, it was striking from school and sitting in front of Swedish parliament with a sign saying, "school strike for climate". She inspired a global school-strike movement and challenged world leaders to take action on climate change. Little actions can grow into big movements. Never be afraid to start small.

Building goals

The time has come to visualise your highest self – the future version of you that is flourishing, glowing, happy, at peace and purposeful. Yes, your goals can be about your education or your career, but you don't have to limit your vision to those things. Visualise what you want your health or fitness to be like or the quality of your friendships; maybe there's a hobby you want to pick up or a country you would love to travel to.

Activity time
Vision board

You can start by simply writing down your ideas and goals, but I encourage you to go a step further and create a vision board – a visual reminder of everything you are working towards and believe in. A vision board is a collage of photos, magazine clippings, quotes and affirmations that represent your goals. You could use a large sheet of paper or cardboard and glue down images and words that inspire your vision! It could be even more fun to host a vision board party for your friends.

Vision board supplies:
- Your mission statement or list of goals
- Scissors
- Magazines or newspapers to cut things out of
- Glue
- Felt-tips or markers
- Paper or cardboard

Optional:
- Yummy snacks to nibble on
- Inspiring or motivational playlist

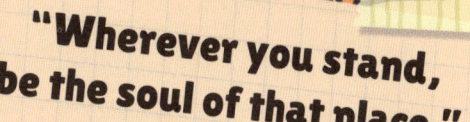

"Wherever you stand, be the soul of that place."
Rumi

Step into your power

No more shrinking. No more hiding. Walk into the room, cool, calm and ready to take your place at the table or shake things up and create your own. Send the world a message to say you are confident, open to opportunities, authentically yourself, armed with knowledge and unashamed.

As you continue to exercise your newfound power and potential, you may find yourself in rooms, spaces and places where you are the 'only one'. This could be because of your age, gender, race, abilities, family background or maybe a combination of all these aspects of your identity. It may feel weird and uncomfortable, but know that this is part of taking up space and being the person you feel called to be. It may feel lonely sometimes but remind yourself of all

the incredible people who have also walked the lonely path to freedom, change or influence. Continue spending time with yourself and those who nurture, encourage and challenge you to be better. Explore your potential, get a range of experiences under your belt, say yes to opportunities that serve your goals and radically believe in your abilities. You are a force of nature – limitless in potential.

Remember, you are not alone . . . but part of a global group of people taking up space.

WE ARE ALL ROOTING FOR YOU!

Useful resources

Books

You Don't Understand Me: Finding Yourself, Facing Your Problems, and Figuring Out Life (When Nobody Gets it), Dr Tara Porter (2022)

Banish Your Self-Esteem Thief: A Cognitive Behavioural Therapy Workbook on Building Positive Self-Esteem for Young People, Katie Collins-Donnelly (2014)

Grown: The Black Girls' Guide to Glowing Up, Melissa Cummings-Quarry and Natalie Carter (2021)

Welcome to Consent: How to Say No, When to Say Yes and Everything in Between, Yumi Stynes and Dr Melissa Kang (2021)

Websites and phone numbers

Chapter 1 – Identity
NSPCC: www.nspcc.org.uk (0808 800 5000)
Young Minds: www.youngminds.org.uk/young-person (0808 802 5544)

Chapter 5 – Mind, Mood and Feelings
Mind: www.mind.org.uk (0300 102 1234)
Samaritans: www.samaritans.org (116 123)
Rethink Mental Illness: www.rethink.org (0808 801 0525)
British Association for Counselling and Psychotherapy: www.bacp.co.uk
The Counselling Foundation: www.counsellingfoundation.org

Chapter 6 – School
WCAN: www.wcan.uk
Bright Network: www.brightnetwork.co.uk (0207 197 9902)
Aleto Foundation: www.aletofoundation.org.uk
Migrant Leaders: www.migrantleaders.org.uk
Not Fine in School: www.notfineinschool.co.uk/young-people

Chapter 7 – Beliefs
They Work for You: www.theyworkforyou.com
Global Issues: www.globalissues.org
The Prince's Trust: www.princes-trust.org.uk
Centre for Women's Justice: www.centreforwomensjustice.org.uk/timeline

Chapter 8 – The Internet
Young Minds: www.youngminds.org.uk/young-person/coping-with-life/social-media-and-mental-health/ (0808 802 5544)
UK Safer Internet Centre: www.saferinternet.org.uk/guide-and-resource/young-people/resources-for-11-19s
Childnet: www.childnet.com/young-people/
Childline: www.childline.org.uk/info-advice/bullying-abuse-safety/online-mobile-safety/
National Bullying Helpline: www.nationalbullyinghelpline.co.uk/cyberbullying.html (0300 323 0169)

Chapter 9 – Your Safety
Relationships
Rape crisis: www.rapecrisis.org.uk (0808 500 2222)
Women's Aid: www.womensaid.org.uk (0208 554 9004)
The Survivor's Trust: www.thesurvivorstrust.org (0808 801 0818)

Family
Childline: https://www.nspcc.org.uk/keeping-children-safe/our-services/childline/ (0800 1111)
Rights 4 Children: www.rights4children.org.uk
Family Lives: www.familylives.org.uk (0808 800 2222)

Bullying
National Bullying Helpline: https://www.nationalbullyinghelpline.co.uk/kids.html (0300 323 0169)

Crime
Fearless: www.fearless.org (0800 555 111)

Acknowledgements

For every idea that manages to escape the busy thought-life of an author and find its resting place in the pages of a book, there is a community of passionate, supportive souls that make it possible. I use this opportunity to acknowledge and appreciate some of these special people.

I want to thank my daughter Esme for being my biggest inspiration and the best writing buddy. You were womb-side when I started working on this book, but you are now safely in my arms as I complete it. I hope you enjoy reading it in the years to come.

To my awesome husband Gbemi, thank you. For your affirming words and sacrificial efforts in creating a space where I could focus, think, research and write with ease. I appreciate you.

Mum, Dad, Timothy and Emmanuel – my core, my very people. Through life's many transitions, thank you for always believing and always encouraging.

To the stellar team at Little Tiger – special thanks to Isabel Otter, my ever-patient, intuitive and genius editor. Thank you for trudging through countless drafts and offering fresh ideas with each round. Working with you has been the best experience. Thank you, Soofiya and Lila Cruz – you have blown us away with your vibrant and fun illustrations, and thank you to Emma Jennings, Maddie Pilkington and Meg Chadderton for the exceptional cover and interior design. To Beth Cox and Lisa Davis for enriching this project with your expertise on inclusion and diversity. Thank you all; your work has made all the difference.

To every brave young person who has trusted me with their precious stories and life experiences over the years, I say thank you. While it has been my privilege to serve and support you, you have taught me so much about hope and resilience. Together, I hope we will continue to learn, heal and grow.